LEADERSHIP RECOGNITION OF ORGANIZATIONAL CITIZENSHIP BEHAVIORS IN PERFORMANCE EVALUATIONS IN WASHINGTON STATE HEALTHCARE ORGANIZATIONS

A Research Study

JULIE D. GRIFFIN CONZELMANN, D.M.

Author: **Julia Griffin Conzelmann, D.M.**
Camano Island, WA 98282; julie.conzelmann@gmail.com

Publisher: **Dawn D. Boyer, M.Ad.Ed., Ph.D.**
Virginia Beach, VA 23464; Dawn.Boyer@me.com

Copyright © Original Dissertation 2012; Commercial Conversion 2015

ISBN Numbers ISBN-13: 978-1517140328
ISBN-10: 1517140323

Disclaimer:

The author has attempted to gather as much of the facts and information to the utmost complete and truthfulness for the compilation of this book from bona fide sources, internet sources, printed material in currently circulating and non-circulating sources, newspaper articles, peer reviewed journal articles, and personal interviews. Dates noted were from publically available sources or as noted during the course of the study.

Keep in mind – if any data included (or left out, incorrectly quoted, or attributed), it may be attributed to transcription errors or types. Several bodies of research were interpretations of the same or original documents and errors might have occurred as transcribed. Material or resources mentioned or offered data that seemingly 'fit' or matched other known and documented facts. Anyone with more data to contribute to a future, updated, and corrected version of this project is encouraged to send materials to the author's point of contact noted within this book.

Connect to the Author

Julie.conzelmann@gmail.com
Business Website: http://www.superioreditingservices.com
LinkedIn Profile: https://www.linkedin.com/in/juliegriffin1
Facebook Business Page: https://www.facebook.com/superioreditingservices
Twitter: http://www.Twitter.com/Dr_Conzelmann

Leadership Recognition Of Organizational Citizenship Behaviors In Performance Evaluations In Washington State Healthcare Organizations

by

JULIE DIANE GRIFFIN, D.M.

A Dissertation Presented in Partial Fulfillment
of the Requirements for the Degree
Doctor of Management – Organizational Leadership

UNIVERSITY OF PHOENIX

August 2012

William O'Donnell, Ph.D., Committee Chair
Nancy Kennedy, Ph.D., Committee Member
T. Lee Burnham, Ph.D., Committee Member

Accepted and Signed: _____ 07/20/2012
William O'Donnell   Date

Accepted and Signed: _____ 07/20/2012
Nancy Kennedy   Date

Accepted and Signed: _____ 07/20/2012
T. Lee Burnham   Date

_____ 08/09/2012
Jeremy Moreland, Ph.D.   Date
Executive Dean, School of Advanced Studies

This text has been altered in format from the original dissertation document to conform to easier to read format for the general public and commercial publishing standards. Scholars reviewing the contents and formatting should not model any thesis or dissertation after this book's current formatting. See your school's individual research study guidelines for formatting for the graduate level thesis or dissertation.

Copyright, 2015, Julie D. Griffin Conzelmann, D.M.

TABLE OF CONTENTS

LIST OF TABLES

DEDICATION & ACKNOWLEDGEMENTS

I want to make a special mention of love and gratitude to my mother, Beulah Elisabeth (McGinnis) Olsen (1940 – 1996): A beautiful soul who told me I could do and be whatever I put my mind, heart, and soul into.

My family has been the most important relationship throughout this entire journey. Therefore, I dedicate this work and extend my deepest appreciation to the love of my life, Eric Conzelmann, whose love inspired me to do well and focus on the finish line. I also wish to recognize my family and friends, for the love and support throughout this awesome educational and personal journey of growth, and for sacrificing time and effort as life went on around me, and without me, in it.

I want to acknowledge the contributions and support of my mentor and committee chair, Dr. William "Billyo!" O'Donnell, for offering to mentor anyone from the 2008 University of Phoenix Masters program who applied to the UOPX doctoral program, keeping his word, and assisting me through my doctoral journey and my dissertation. I also wish to extend gratitude to Dr. Nancy Kennedy and Dr. T. Lee Burnham for their input, patience, and assistance as my committee members for my dissertation process. Yes, Dr. Kennedy, we were a great team!

Additional acknowledgements for their constructive criticism, general feedback, and extension of knowledge during my doctoral residencies go to Dr. Gene Jablonski (1st year), Dr. Timothy Delicath (2nd year), and the tag-team ladies Dr. Louise Underdahl and Dr. Suzann Beier, who stepped in at the last minute for an ill colleague – and for which many students were more grateful than you will ever know (3rd year)!

I wish to acknowledge Dr. William Fournier, Assistant Professor at Marietta College in Ohio, who provided me permission to use his validated survey instrument to create the survey document for this dissertation. I also wish to give a huge thank you to

Dr. Tom Granoff at La Sierra University, California, for his exemplary guidance and assistance with the statistical analysis and discussion of the data for my survey.

I wonder where I would be now without my UOPX doctoral co-learners: John Wilcox, Theresa Villorente, and Trish Shail-Berryman! Together we were the Fab Four and Team A for so many of our doctoral courses together. Thank you J, T, and T for your feedback, sharing your ideas, and always letting me lead the challenge through each team assignment. I learned so much from each of you, and I will always cherish the laughs, the tears, the hugs, and our team photo from third-year residency December 3-10, 2010, in Phoenix, Arizona.

JULIE DIANE GRIFFIN CONZELMAN, D.M

FOREWARD

I chose to pursue the topic of organizational citizenship behaviors when I realized my colleagues and I performed tasks outside the realm of our job descriptions, but received no recognition or compensation from leadership. I performed an experiment over the span of one year. Every time my direct supervisor gave me an assignment outside the basic scope of my position I wrote the task on a list.

At the time of my annual performance evaluation, I appended my list to my paperwork – which my supervisor immediately ripped off and threw in the trash – exclaiming no other documentation could be appended to the paperwork! I filed a complaint with the human resources department and discovered my additional information was more than welcome to substantiate my statements and perspective regarding the scope of my performance.

My boss offered me a 1.8% raise; my boss's boss, the division vice president, changed that to a 3.2% raise based on my additional information! Interestingly, the Division Vice President recognized my extra work, and provided me with several letters and cash awards for going 'above and beyond.'

If these 'extras' were incentive enough for me to perform better, become more team-oriented, and enjoy my job, I wanted to discover if other people realized a benefit from their managers or organization, call it a 'pat on the back,' or some other form of recognition, during their annual performance reviews for going above and beyond.

ABSTRACT

LEADERSHIP RECOGNITION OF ORGANIZATIONAL CITIZENSHIP BEHAVIORS IN PERFORMANCE EVALUATIONS IN WASHINGTON STATE HEALTHCARE ORGANIZATIONS

Studies in the social sciences over the past three decades provided a forum in which to further research organizational citizenship behaviors (OCBs) in the workplace. Organizational Citizenship Behaviors (OCBs) are defined by Kinicki and Kreitner (2007) as "employee behaviors that exceed work-role requirements" (p. 167). The study of organizational citizenship behaviors in all industries continues to emerge.

To further the subject of OCBs, this study measured the perception of leadership recognition and rewards in relation to exhibiting OCBs among employees who work in the healthcare industry in Washington State. Qualifying participants completed a study through random, voluntary completion of written surveys at a retail store in a town based in Washington State and a secure, web-based survey site.

The results of the quantitative analysis indicated the majority of respondents exhibited citizenship-type behaviors and leaders did not adequately recognize or reward these behaviors. The findings revealed satisfaction, performance, teamwork, and productivity increased significantly when OCBs are exhibited, recognized, and rewarded. The statistical analysis supported previous research on OCB, establishing a positive relationship among leadership recognition and rewards of OCBs, satisfaction, performance, teamwork, and productivity.

CHAPTER I

INTRODUCTION

The subject of organizational leadership understanding the human resources tools available to run a successful organization is difficult, especially regarding leaders recognizing the contributions of employees in the performance evaluation process in organizations. Many organizations lack formal processes to recognize the value-added to an organization and employee performance by employees who exhibit Organizational Citizenship Behaviors (OCBs) in addition to those tasks and other behaviors organizations expect as part of generic job descriptions at the time of hiring employees. OCBs are defined by Kinicki and Kreitner (2007) as "employee behaviors that exceed work-role requirements" (p. 167), and described as individual mood, actions, and reactions exhibited by employees influenced by the ability to be autonomous (Smith,

Organ, & Near, 1983). The research by Smith, Organ, and Near (1983) and Kinicki and Kreitner (2007) supported the argument a correlation exists between the OCBs exhibited by employees and the improved productivity, job satisfaction, and increased productivity, and retention of employees.

Organizations must adapt to proven management theories to continue successfully to attain organizational goals. A review of the literature about OCB over the past several decades suggested growing implementation of behavioral management theories, such as design science increases employee productivity and job satisfaction; therefore increasing organizational profits (Van Aken, 2007). Management must recognize the value-added by employee behaviors, besides those listed as part of generic job descriptions and titles as provided upon hiring employees. A literature review found the most notable definition of OCB is as part of social exchange theory (Emerson, 1976).[1] Future research into designing and implementing processes recognizing OCB through relationships between employees and supervisors

---

[1] Defined in chapter 2 under Leadership Theories: "Social exchange...is limited to actions that are contingent on rewarding reactions from others" (Emerson, 1976, p. 336).

may be helpful in attaining organizational goals. Some ways to accomplish organizational goals is to recognize how OCB affects relationships between employees and supervisors – one of the more powerful employment relationships affecting organizational processes. The creation of job standardization processes may be necessary to increase productivity, teamwork, job performance, and job satisfaction. The increase in productivity, teamwork, job performance, and job satisfaction may support the argument the employee and organizational benefits are cost-effective and can affect positive, long-term organizational productivity.

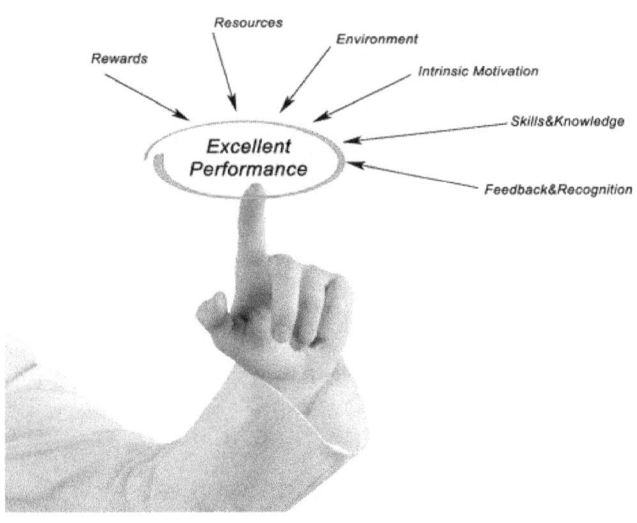

Background of the Problem

Organizations recruit or promote employees who can perform the activities for the successful operation of the organization. The basis for making a decision to employ one candidate over another in a specific position are the qualifications to perform the duties of the position, but does not include the extent to which an employee may exhibit OCB. Part of the leadership focus on knowledge, skills, and abilities (KSAs) includes how leadership relates KSAs to OCBs. From the findings revealed in the supporting literature, leaders should focus on implementing a formal process to include personal experiences, training, and education as part of the hiring, retention, and reward practices in organizations. Prospective employees receive a description of required tasks and duties, but no information regarding additional intrinsic behaviors that may add to the successful completion of job performance. Some leaders have a difficult time determining the best candidates to hire. Leaders who do not understand the recruiting process may lead to an increase in the disparity of the requisite knowledge, skills, and abilities (KSAs) employees bring to the organization. The recruiting process does not normally provide the organization with information about any OCB candidates may exhibit as employees with the organization. Organizations can better identify discrepancies in skill sets to perform specific tasks in specific areas or industries by recognizing the benefit of formally recognizing and rewarding employees who exhibit traits of OCB.

When employees engage in OCB and leaders provide reward or recognition, employees feel good about themselves. Fournier (2008) posited that leadership recognition of the exhibition of OCBs by employees has a positive effect on the perception of equality and fairness from leaders. In return for the perception of fair treatment, employee turnover decreases, and employee satisfaction and morale increase. Citing Adams' equity theory (1965), Fournier also indicated the lack of recognition of OCB increases symptoms of employee negativity, such as anger, resentment, absenteeism, theft, an increase in turnover, and a decline of employees' mental and physical health.

Mathis and Jackson (2006) stated that "organizations retain or lose employees based on five drivers of retention: job design and work, career opportunities, characteristics of the organization, relationships, and rewards" (p. 81). A good job match between the individual KSAs and the balance of work and family life is a reason organizations seem to be successful in retaining employees. The opportunity for professional and personal growth is also a positive determinant of employee retention. The relationship that employees build by working within teams in organizations also builds trust and loyalty, thus increasing an employee's desire to work for the organization.

The number one reason most employees leave organizations is the lack of adequate rewards and benefits – as perceived by the employee (Mathis & Jackson, 2006). The employee who perceives a disparity in the performance of other employees compared to personal job performance may exit the organization and look for employment elsewhere. Organizations may increase employee retention by linking performance management and the performance evaluation process to pay increases and employee recognition processes (Mathis & Jackson, 2006, p. 87).

Many organizations use a performance appraisal process to identify area of efficiencies and inefficiencies within the organization. Performance appraisals are results-based, rating employees based on completing tasks and meeting strategic goals. The results of performance reviews may stimulate an increase in employee performance and justify the need to change employee salaries. Employees perceive performance appraisals as a way to weed out the strongest and weakest performers, and as a tool for leaders to promote or terminate employees (Mathis & Jackson, 2006; Kreitner, 2004). Results-based performance evaluations are necessary, including a trait and behaviorally focused section within the performance evaluation process, which can assist with the individualization of performance reviews.

According to Willer, Lovaglia, and Markovsky (1997) individual traits such as attitude, initiative, and creativity, coupled with individual behaviors of mood, altruism, influence, and emotion can and should be part of OCB, and recognized as influencing employee motivation to attain personal and organizational goals and objectives.

From a leadership perspective, OCB goes beyond the formal job task requirements for which leaders measure employee performance. OCB is sometimes an unnoticeable action making the behavior and action difficult to measure to have any influence on future performance evaluations (Mathis & Jackson, 2006, p. 332). The research concluded a relationship exists between leadership support and recognition of OCBs (Johnson, 2008, p. 6). Because no metrics exist for recognizing and measuring employee exhibition of OCB, prior research by Willer, Lovaglia, and Markovsky (1997) and Mathis & Jackson (2006) suggested an opportunity existed to determine an effective way to recognize and reward OCB in performance evaluations.

Statement of the Problem

Chen, Niu, Wang, Yang, and Tsaur (2009) cited Katz (1964) in defining Organizational Citizenship Behaviors (OCB) as "individual behavior that is discretionary" (p. 39) and not part of the formal job performance evaluation and recognition process of the organization. Lack of recognition in performance evaluations by leaders appears to negatively affect productivity of employees exhibiting OCB in Washington State healthcare organizations. Organizational leaders lack a formal process to recognize and reward the value-added by employees who exhibit OCB. Organizational citizenship behaviors are those behaviors leaders expect employees to perform as part of generic job descriptions and titles as provided by human resources at the time of hire (Kinicki & Kreitner, 2006).

This quantitative research study identified positions with highly complicated and specific skills required for organizations to succeed and compared this with the OCB skills exhibited by the employees who stated they held these position levels. It was determined leadership recognition of OCBs and performance above the listed job duties added to the benefit of the organizations' attainment of strategic goals. Some organizations may already use some form of human resources software to track employee KSAs and performance. If so, updating the organizational database may help identify employees with the required KSAs for specific jobs and create an OCB database to track and match the progress of leadership recognition and rewards.

The elements of the selected design were descriptive and quantitative because the variables in the study required only one instance of measurement during the research project to assess any association between the elements and OCBs (Black, 2005). The specific elements were employee productivity, teamwork, job satisfaction, job performance, and the rewards and recognition processes for the organization in implementing formal recognition and reward processes in job performance evaluations for employees who exhibit OCB. Employee productivity, teamwork, job satisfaction, cost, and rate of turnover are measurable; an analysis of the information obtained from organizations helped determine the recognition or lack of recognition of OCBs.

Purpose of the Study

The purpose of this descriptive, quantitative study was to analyze the benefits of formally recognizing employees who exhibited OCBs as part of the formal performance evaluation process. A random sample of 115 employees representing each of 10 various healthcare industries in Washington State determined whether leadership recognition of OCB positively affected employee productivity, teamwork, job satisfaction, and resulting rewards. Smith, Organ, and Near (1983) suggested employee compliance and altruism are behaviors that affect whether employees exhibit OCBs. Organizational citizenship behaviors are independent variables that may change as employees are or are not productive, satisfied, or actively participating in team-based projects (Smith et al. 1983; Steinberg, 2008). Leadership, peer mood, and feedback are important control variables, and included as influential and motivational tools for employees to exhibit OCBs (George & Zhou, 2007).

During the review of the literature, no information revealed any organizations directly or explicitly recognized OCBs as part of the formal reward and recognition system. Designing and implementing a performance evaluation process that officially recognizes the value of OCB would be beneficial to most organizations, according to a study by Johnson, Holladay, and Quinones (2009). An employee perception that OCB is an expectation of job performance exists (Chen et al., 2009; Chen & Chiu, 2009). Johnson et al. (2009) stated employees who exhibit OCBs have a good faith expectation of a reward for increased contributions, even though the employer is not contractually obligated to provide any pay or benefits over the agreed compensation or pay-for-performance rate during the employment tenure. This perception and expectation may come from the added term to official employee task documentation as *other duties as assigned*. This subject requires more research regarding the cost benefit and improvement of implementing operational systems for formally recognizing and rewarding employees who exhibit OCBs in organizations.

Significance of the Problem.

The literature regarding important
organizational leadership theories and practices that
may affect OCB is plentiful. General systems theory
(Von Bertalanffy, 1972) is the process of identifying,
processing, and resolving organizational issues,
included leader-follower relationships surrounding
performance rewards and benefits. Literature
regarding organizational design theories and
behaviors is readily available, such as models and
strategies to increase organizational performance and
employee satisfaction (Galbraith, 1974). A gap does
exist between how the leadership theories,
organizational design, and organizational behavior
theories contributed to employees exhibiting or
leaders recognizing OCB. Chiaburu, Oh, Berry, Ling,
and Gardner (2011) reported organizations that hire
employees because of the propensity to exhibit OCBs
could create lasting benefits to stakeholders,
organizations, employees, vendors, and global
societies. Organizational citizenship behavior is part
of the basis of the social exchange theory proposed

by Emerson (1976). Emerson (1976) stated prior literature over several decades that revealed employees exhibited OCB wherein the organization received a benefit and the employees anticipated receiving a benefit for the effort.

Significance of the Study.

Providing solutions for organizational issues is necessary and needs further research for the optimum success of organizations. Leaders must decide whether to recognize and reward employees for outstanding job performance. Using societal and demographical information is helpful for identifying plans for implementation. Organizational leaders must be ready to recognize and reward employees for personal and organizational successes. Succession planning is extremely important to the success of organizations (Schiffbauer, Barrett O'Brien, Timmons, & Kiarie, 2008). By selecting the best skilled employees for promotional opportunities, especially those who exhibit OCB to a high degree, leaders can mentor employees over time within the organization. The identification of leadership mentees allows for the

selection and training of the future leaders of the
organization while sustaining the continuity of
business performance and lowering the stress of
change among organizational management.

Organizations depend on hiring employees to
perform necessary tasks enabling the organizations to
reach strategic goals. Organizations should strive to
hire employees with the knowledge, skills, abilities,
experience, and education to produce and sell goods
and services at a profit to the organization to attain
organizational strategic goals. A disparity may exist in
the selection and placement of employees regarding
the KSAs and the OCBs the employees may exhibit.
Because of the lack of recognition and rewards
processes regarding employee performance,
additional duties that are not included as part of the
official tasks of the position during hire may not
become part of daily employee performance.

Significance of the Study to Leadership.

Summers, Boje, Dennehy, and Rosile (1997)
stated, "Organizations that learn and understand how
the organization functions on the most basic internal

and behavioral level can apply such knowledge toward improving an organization's effectiveness" (p. 347). Organizational citizenship behaviors are important to business management leadership because organizations may be forced to downsize full-time employees (FTEs). Organizations rely on quality research regarding organizational staffing decisions for successful operation of organizations. Organizational leaders may learn how to recognize and reward the performance of employees and rate employees who exhibit OCBs through a valid research study. By providing valid research perspectives from subject experts, organizational leaders may be open to assistance more so than not acquiring information based on sound research.

Nature of the Study.

The method of obtaining the quantitative data for the study was to identify organizations that do or do not formally recognize OCB as part of employee performance evaluations. After receiving permission for organizational participation, a survey used a random sample of 115 anonymous employees representing each of 10 various healthcare industries in Washington State. The participants included employees holding management and non-management positions that provided both a leadership and non-leadership perspective of OCB recognition in the workplace. The survey instrument was a modified, valid document approved and published in a dissertation by Fournier (2008) (Appendix A), and the information requested was similar and consistent to the information to complete this study. The survey requested a personal assessment of individual participant KSAs, education, experience, OCB, and rating recent job satisfaction. Participants provided a list of OCBs exhibited. The human resources departments for several healthcare organizations were asked to provide a detailed job description and a list of required KSAs for each position to assist in creating the survey, but all declined to participate in the study.

The selection of participants and organizations commenced by first securing Institutional Review Board (IRB) certification to work with human subjects (Appendix B), and asking for permission to recruit random volunteers through several medical organization's human resources department. Leaders from the medical organizations declined to approve the request, but permission was obtained to conduct the survey in the parking lot of a local retail store. The informed consent document (Appendix C) provided participants an understanding of the expectations and parameters of the study, and the participant withdrawal form (Appendix D) allowed participants the ability to withdraw from the study at any time, for any reason with the assurance of confidentiality.

The data analysis included the resulting organizational and participant information by whether the organization formally recognizes OCB or has no formal recognition of OCB. The individual participant analysis included a data sort according to OCBs, KSAs, education, experience, teamwork, and job satisfaction ratings. One possible outcome of this study was to determine whether employees' perception of OCB recognition increased productivity, teamwork, and job satisfaction. This will make it possible to compare recent trends and may suggest a direction for future research.

The need to research, validate, and improve systems to identify the best qualified employees for specific organizations is important to doctoral studies as the world of business and direction of organizations change. As these global changes in business occur, the most up-to-date, valid, and reliable research provides data and solutions on issues facing organizations. The ability to identify opportunities for improving organizational human resources benefits, identify future leadership needs, and set the stage for future research on OCBs is important for organizational growth.

A study conducted by Schiffbauer et al. (2008 concluded research exists regarding leadership managing and understanding human resources issues in various countries. However, the majority of research available on OCB centers on health-related issues, limiting the usefulness of the research and design in other industries. The analysis and design of a doctoral study regarding OCB should have the flexibility to be useful in any organizational setting.

A sound doctoral study provides information for the need for changes in Enterprise Resource Planning (ERP). Enterprise Resource Planning includes performing a workforce analysis, environmental analysis, strategic planning, goal setting, benchmarking, and best practices specifically in critical roles in healthcare. The ideal outcome of further research will be to determine if the recognition of OCB is beneficial to organizations. If the outcome is positive organizational leaders should design and implement a study that provides an outcome specifying a valid, reliable, and optimum solution for bettering the organizational leadership's recognition of OCBs in the performance review process. This information may be part of expert subject as future foundational doctoral research.

Overview of the Research Method.

To determine if implementing an organizational recognition and rewards process regarding employees who exhibit OCBs as part of the official tasks of employees, a quantitative study was a research method. Sometimes a qualitative research studies have provided the same results as a quantitative study; however, it was determined a long description of relevant variables was not the best method to distribute and describe the information (Steinberg, 2008). A quantitative study provides more in-depth results using the nominal, Likert-type scale (Steinberg, 2008) a universal and measurable method. A mathematical comparison of the quantitative data for the variables assisted in determining the probability of if the research data supported the research question. A comparison of the data from a quantitative perspective also uncovered other relevant information for further research on the subject in a way not found through qualitative research.

The independent variables for this quantitative research study were:

a) Altruism: the intrinsic desire to do the right thing
b) Compliance: 'good citizen' syndrome (Smith, et al., 1983)

For this quantitative study the dependent variables, according to Steinberg (2008) were:

a) Productivity
b) Teamwork
c) Job satisfaction

d) Job performance

e) Rewards and recognition

For this quantitative study the control variables were:

a) Mood (as a motivator) (George & Zhou, 2007)

b) Feedback

With the possibility of testing more than one hypothesis, lopsided testing may have increased the validity of the results to either accept or reject the hypothesis, which may have led to the incorrect conclusion for the research question.

Overview of the Design Appropriateness.

In designing the study parameters, a qualitative study was not appropriate for the subject of OCB as the individual interpretation of verbal questions and responses may have become subjective in the translation during the data analysis. The translation problem may have increased the incidence of perceptive bias in reporting the data and skewed the results. A quantitative study provided a mathematical summation of employee perspectives of the recognition of OCBs from survey questions, and allowed an objective, and concise discussion of the survey results. A quantitative study answered one research question and tested one hypothesis to determine if a correlation existed between leadership and employees' perceptions of OCB recognition. The study determined that formal recognition and rewards included as part of the employee evaluation process increased employee productivity, performance, teamwork, and job satisfaction.

Description of Research Focus

Performance standards consider basic performance criterion, quantity of output, the quality of output, time management, attendance, and teamwork. The lack of individual contributions when providing performance evaluations excludes the additional contributions employees provide that may enhance the successful attainment of organizational goals and objectives. Unmotivated employees are less likely to be attentive, productive, and satisfied at work

(Fournier, 2008). The organization may suffer the consequences through missed deadlines, inadequate product, and increased costs. For the benefit of organizations, regarding employee contributions based on employees who exhibit OCBs as part of the performance evaluation process, the research study proposed these research question and hypothesis:

Research Question.

Q^1: What effect does leadership recognition of OCBs in performance evaluations have on employees' productivity, teamwork, job performance, and satisfaction?

Hypothesis.

H^1: There is an increase in productivity, teamwork, job performance, and satisfaction because of implementing a formal process of recognizing and rewarding employees for exhibiting OCB as part of the employee evaluation process.

Null Hypothesis.

H°: There is no increase in productivity, teamwork, job performance, and satisfaction because of implementing a formal process of recognizing and rewarding employees for exhibiting OCB as part of the employee evaluation process.

The objective was to ensure the research considered the areas of influence, such as altruism, mood, emotions, and individual motivation while staying within the specific direction proposed in the problem statement (Cooper & Schindler, 2002).

Theoretical Framework

Past literature on OCB has a foundation from several theoretical practices, such as participative management theory (Collins (1997), motivational, transformational, and situational leadership theories (Yukl, 2010), and human resources management (HRM), planning, and behaviors (Rosen, Berger, & Tarcher, 1991). The most significant theoretical area that OCB falls under is social exchange theory, broadly defined as actions initiated by one person with a possible expectation of a receiving a reward for performing the action (Emerson, 1976). When an organization hires an employee an exchange of need and benefit occurs: the organization needs an employee to perform a task, and the employee benefits through receiving compensation for performing the task. Emerson (1976) cited Burgess and Nelsen's (1974) study of operant reinforcement (p. 337) compared to employment concepts. The social exchange concept benefits organizations through resources, rewards, and reinforcement (employees, pay, performance reviews); the benefit to employees and organizations are opportunity, growth, and profit.

Using the concepts derived from the social exchange theory, collecting data from an employee perspective was necessary to answer the research question and hypothesis of if increased productivity, teamwork, job performance, and satisfaction is noticeable because of implementing a formal process of recognizing and rewarding employees for exhibiting OCB as part of the employee evaluation process. The study addressed the addition of two independent variables and two control variables. The independent and control variables were intrinsic, emotional motivators varying among individuals. These intrinsic motivators may have increased the successful outcome of the research study to support the research question and hypothesis:

a) Independent variables (IV): altruism and compliance

b) Dependent variables (DV): productivity, teamwork, job satisfaction, performance, and recognition and rewards

c) Control variables (CV): mood and feedback

The independent variables of altruism and compliance are inherent individual behaviors. Altruism is an inherent behavior influenced by mood and emotions (Willer et al., 1997). For example, an employee who arrives at work after an argument with a spouse the night before may be irritable and exhibit a negative mood and attitude toward performing job tasks. Compliance with requests to perform tasks may be affected by employee moods and emotions as well (Willer et al., 1997).

The dependent variables of productivity, teamwork, job performance, job satisfaction, and rewards depended on individualistic perceived value by employees in relation to rewards and recognition (Mathis & Jackson, 2006). Some employees may view the performance evaluation process as a way to assess individual contributions in a negative way in rating individual performance. Kreitner (2004) suggested performance appraisals focus on basic job tasks and standard rating systems. Mathis and Jackson (2006) argued standardizing performance appraisals creates room for rating errors and bias, and excluded rewarding the individual contributions of employees. The control variables of mood and feedback affected research data results based on information provided by participants in relation to the question regarding recent performance evaluations.

Outliers are variables with little or no difference on the outcome of a study (Steinberg, 2008). Any outlying data would be necessary information to have included in the statistical data to show consideration for the variables as part of the research and testing process. Including any outlying information also may have provided validity and reliability to the tests.

However, no outlier information was identified during the data collection process. The minimum statistical methods for a quantitative study are multiple-regression analysis, ANOVA, a descriptive analysis, and a covariance analysis, to determine if any independent or dependent variables affected any identified control variables. Tables were provided for reviewing the data, analysis methods, and outcomes.

The study requirements included capturing data from 115 employees representing each of 10 various healthcare industries in Washington State. Calculation and determination of the sample population size followed a formula recommended by Tabachnick and Fidell (2001, p. 117):

Sample Size = $104 + m$, where m equals the number of independent variables. The results of the survey assisted in determining that OCB is not recognized and the employees were aware of exhibiting OCB as part of normal job tasks. The analysis of the data required using various forms of statistical analysis to determine if any independent or dependent variables existed to answer the research question. The results from the analysis assisted with

supporting the hypotheses and rejecting the null
hypothesis.

Definition of Terms

The following terms are noted to assist the
reader with acronyms and definitions used within the
study:

Enterprise Resource Planning (ERP) –
Enterprise Resource Planning includes performing a
workforce analysis, environmental analysis, strategic
planning, goal setting, benchmarking, and best
practices specifically in critical roles in healthcare.

Interactional Justice – George and Zhou (2007)
defined interactional justice as leaders involving
employees in the decision-making process so
information is readily available and modeling how to
react effectively to decisions (p. 608).

Knowledge, Skills, and Abilities (KSAs) – KSAs
are qualification standards describing the minimum
requirements necessary to perform work of a

particular occupation successfully and safely. These minimum requirements may include specific job-related work experience, education, medical or physical standards, training, security, and/or licensure. They are not designed to rank candidates, identify the best qualified for a particular position, or substitute for an analysis of an applicant's knowledge, skills, and abilities/competencies (Office of Personnel Management, 2015).

Organizational Citizenship Behavior (OCB) – Dennis Organ is generally considered the father of OCB. Organ expanded upon Katz's (1964) original work. Organ (1988) defines OCB as "individual behavior that is discretionary, not directly or explicitly recognized by the formal reward system, and that in the aggregate promotes the effective functioning of the organization" (p. 4). Organ's definition of OCB includes three critical aspects that are central to this construct. First, OCBs are thought of as discretionary behaviors, which are not part of the job description, and are performed by the employee as a result of personal choice. Second, OCBs go above and beyond that which is an enforceable requirement of the job description. Finally, OCBs contribute positively to overall organizational effectiveness (Organ, 2006).

Procedural Justice – Procedural justice refers to the perception of fairness one feels when one considers the process used by leaders to make decisions (Fournier, 2008).

Assumptions

One assumption regarding recognizing and rewarding employees who exhibit OCBs is the employees may continue to exhibit the behaviors. A second assumption is as leaders recognize and reward employees for OCB behaviors, other employees may also exhibit the behaviors. Li and Hung (2009) discussed how the social exchange theory related to the influence of leader-follower relationships. The basis of the study by Li and Hung (2009) found leaders used the close leader-follower relationship to elicit OCBs from employees. The employees who exhibited OCBs from the interaction of the leader-follower relationship worked closely with coworkers, "leading to a spillover effect" of which the organization directly benefitted (Li & Hung, 2009, p. 6). Another assumption is OCBs are an expectation of job performance and teamwork and are so well incorporated into the performance evaluation process that leaders do not believe the OCBs should be a consideration separate from the specific required job tasks. Support of these assumptions was not part of the discovery in the study because of the scope of the study and the course of research.

George and Zhou (2007) hypothesized positive and negative moods serve constructive functions within organizations and argued a direct correlation exists between positive and negative moods and an increase in creativity. George and Zhou (2007) also argued a dual interaction between positive and negative moods influenced creativity (p. 606). Colbert (2010) reported conflicting results on whether positive and negative moods foster or reduce creativity. The results of the study supported the argument that positive and negative mood affect individual behavior correlating OCB to creativity (George & Zhou, 2007, p. 607).

The hypothesis that positive and negative
moods interact to promote creativity is part of an
experiment by George and Zhou (2007). The
research showed employees with a positive mood are
less likely to be creative or innovative (George &
Zhou, 2007, p. 607). Conversely, employees
experiencing a negative mood experienced an
elevated ability to focus on specific problems; finding
motivation to instigate problem solving and optimize
strategies (George & Zhou, 2007, p. 608). By using
an example of two employees exhibiting each of the
mood states in a "supportive context" (George &
Zhou, 2007, p. 608) the literature showed leaders will
support subordinates through the process.

By providing developmental feedback,
interactional justice, and extending trust, leaders
increased the possibility employees will exhibit OCB,
be more creative, and innovative, regardless of
whether they succeed or not (George & Zhou, 2007).
Developmental feedback is providing an environment
of shared information that stimulates and motivates
employees to become creative and enjoy the process
of innovation. George and Zhou (2007) defined
interactional justice as leaders involving employees in

the decision-making process so information is readily available and modeling how to react effectively to decisions (p. 608).

A feeling of trust is important for employees to be open, creative, and for leaders to extend the feeling of risk-taking to employees; it is a reciprocal process (George & Zhou, 2007). Without stating leaders should instigate negativity, George and Zhou (2007) concluded "positive and negative moods in combination lead to high levels of creativity in a supportive context suggest both moods are important and valuable" (p. 620) to whether or not employees exhibit OCB.

Human resources leaders define the pay-for-performance on the in-role tasks and activities of particular positions within organizations. Supervisors have access to pay scales within the supervisor's purview and can a set formula of monetary value for specific tasks and roles of each position in the department. Employees who perform *above and beyond* as part of performance of the in-role tasks add value to the bottom-line effectiveness of the organization (Chen & Chiu, 2009). The term *OCB* provides leadership with a new paradigm in changing pay-for-performance discussions in organizations including adding OCB as part of the performance review process and as part of individual- and managerial-based observations.

Li and Hung (2009) investigated the relationship between transformational leadership and OCB using "relationship-based variables" (p. 1,130) instead solely on employee or supervisor perceptions (Chen & Chiu, 2009; Chen et al., 2009; Johnson et al., 2009)). Li and Hung (2009) stated the social-identity and social-exchange relationships forged in performing job duties influenced employees' exhibition of OCB. The relationship between the employee and supervisor influenced employee motivation to continue to exhibit OCB (Li & Hung, 2009). The relationships between supervisors and employees depend on the leadership style, individualized consideration, inspirational motivation, idealized influence, and intellectual stimulation (Li & Hung, 2009). Therefore, the level of OCB exhibited by employees correlate directly with the leadership styles noted by Li and Hung (2009, p. 1138) and vary because of the influence of personality types, possibly moods and individual motivation (Chen & Chiu, 2009; Chen et al., 2009).

The success of organizations depends on performing the individuals recruited and retained by the human resources division. Once known only as the division that processes payroll, the responsibility of many of an organization's success rests on the successful recruitment, hiring, training, and retention of employees. Organizational leaders can increase employee success and retention by focusing on two areas: relationship building and increasing creativity and innovation through behavior management. Both are forms of OCB practices by employees (Sun, Aryee, & Law, 2007; George & Zhou, 2007). A leader, trained through human resources to recognize how

OCB relates to creativity and innovation, may improve the employer/employee relationship important to organizational success (Sun et al., 2007).

Scope

By conducting a study to obtain information regarding perceptions of behaviors, performance, productivity, teamwork, rewards, and recognition from individual employees, organizational leaders need a tool to identify the need for organizational improvements. The study's purpose was to gather data regarding individual perceptions of personal performance, the relationship between employees and leadership, and the expectation of rewards and recognition for individual job performance. Participants working in the healthcare industry in Washington State were asked to provide basic demographic information, to rate personal performance, job satisfaction, communication, and teamwork. Participants were asked to rate the perceived fairness of leadership in providing recognition and rewards in the workplace. After gathering this information, a quantitative data analysis

answered the research question regarding the effect
leadership recognition of OCBs in performance
evaluations has on employees' productivity,
teamwork, job performance, and satisfaction.

Limitations

Some problems anticipated while conducting
this study included the decision to conduct the study
and the decision to use the quantitative over
qualitative method of data analysis. In choosing a
quantitative research design, several limitations of
conducting the study were anticipated. The most
prevalent situations that could have occurred were
selecting an inappropriate group of participants,
inaccurate scoring analysis, or trying to perform the
data analysis with too little information (Neuman,
2003, p. 252). Several anticipated and encountered
problems were the inability to identify and recruit
qualified and willing participants, obtaining too little
data to reach a statistically reliant analysis and
conclusion, not asking for the correct information or
appropriate questions, the possibility of participants
dropping out of the study, and performing the

incorrect data analysis processes, thus potentially skewing the outcome of the data. Additional problems avoided during the study were collecting and using more data than was necessary, subsequently decreasing the opportunity to dilute the results. As part of the data collection process, participants were offered the opportunity to drop out of the study, provide incomplete data, or not return the survey or necessary consent documents. Participants might become preoccupied and need additional prompting to take the survey, extending the time to gather data. With such a broad amount of detail to collect for this study, an additional limitation was determining how much data was necessary for obtaining the most accurate results.

Delimitations

The information obtained in this study did not provide information that placed specific values on OCB, nor did the research exercise study a specific person or unique organization. Discoveries from the study can be a tool for organizations to implement process improvements. Results from this study in no way suggested the ideas or theories in the study are the best information available for organizations. This study was not designed to create new theories, but to expand on ways to use OCB to the best benefit of organizations and human resources needs while providing ideas to increase OCBs through leadership recognition and rewards of OCB through employee performance evaluations.

Summary

In summary, this study encompassed researching various behavioral management theories specifically social exchange theory, as the basis for employees to exhibit OCBs (Emerson, 1976; Li & Hung, 2009). Recognition of OCBs through incorporation into the formal performance review evaluation process may be a catalyst to creating a value-added benefit for both the organization and employees (Li & Hung, 2009). The results of this descriptive and quantitative study determined if implementing OCBs into the formal performance review evaluation process increased productivity, teamwork, job performance, and satisfaction. Adding the control variables as provided by George and Zhou (2007) indicated behaviors and emotions are a factor in employees exhibiting OCBs. This study provided validation that this change may be a cost-effective measure to lower the turnover rate in organizations.

The literature review in chapter two explained the social exchange theory and how the patterns of leadership practices, theories, and performance practices provided affect the leader-follower relationship. The review of historical literature detailed the evolution of OCBs regarding productivity, teamwork, job performance, and satisfaction. The analysis covered different theories of human resources practices and/or management theories. The analysis tied the information into an overview of suggested ways these theories could simultaneously be part of a design plan to implement processes to recognize and reward OCB within many industries and organizations.

CHAPTER II

REVIEW OF LITERATURE

Research into the patterns of human resources practices, theories, and performance practices provided an interesting view into relationships between those with the power to recruit (human resources staff), hire, and retain employees (leaders), and employees. The areas of research for the study included organizational citizenship behavior, social exchange theory, organizational behavior, human resources management (HRM), leadership theory, performance reviews, fairness, and interactional justice. The analysis covered different theories of human resources practices and management theories regarding employee performance reviews. Some of the literature research contributed information about how management practices and theories affected employee motivation and satisfaction regarding the recognition of organizational citizenship behaviors

(OCBs), employee behaviors not required as part of the employee's normal job performance (Kinicki & Kreitner, 2007). Kinicki and Kreitner's research study attempted to tie research by Smith, et al. (1983) to OCBs and determine ways management practices and theories can be part of a design plan to implement recognition and reward processes for employees who exhibit OCBs in healthcare organizations in Washington State.

A literature review of several bodies of research indicated the increasing need to explore, design, and implement job performance pay based on OCBs. Chen and Chiu (2009) theorized an increase in job satisfaction through job redesign also increased motivation and job performance. Chen and Chiu (2009) agreed with the findings of prior research by Brass (1981) and Grant (2008) that job satisfaction is positively correlated to job performance. Job performance is a critical element for the personal psychological status of meaningfulness, responsibility, and results among employees. Vansteenkiste, Neyrinck, Niemiec, Soenens, De Witte, and Van den Broeck (2007, p. 251) stated perceptions of negative work values harmed the psychological need for employees to be competent and motivated at work. The question answered by the research of Chen and Chiu (2009) was that a link existed between OCB and job characteristics as they pertained to in-role and extra-role performance as suggested by Grant (2008) and Boichuk (2010).

Research by Chen et al. (2009) also attempted to separate the stereotypical leadership view of job standardization and making job tasks more routine (p. 45). This makes employee job performance more difficult, time-consuming, and inflexible. The definition of standardization, according to Chen et al. (2009) is the "application of specific, by-the-book, rules and policies that eliminates variation in the same tasks performed by different people" (p. 45). Employee motivation to perform efficiently may increase by implementing strict operating procedures. Managers should design the new procedures to induce OCB and outline the decrease in costs associated with the increase in employees exhibiting OCB (Chen et al., 2009). The program design should include recognition and inclusion of ideas from Li and Hung's (2009) social-exchange theory regarding how employee and supervisor relationships positively affect OCB.

A study led by Johnson et al. (2009) explored employee perceptions of adding OCB as a weighted part of job performance evaluations. The study indicated employees were in agreement OCB should be recognized by leadership as part of a performance evaluation process. The statistical results also indicated employees believe circa 25% of employees' job performance evaluations should recognize employee performance over *and above* the tasks employees normally perform. Employees also stated an expectation that organizations already include OCB as a standard part of the performance evaluation process (p. 409). As part of implementing a new job performance evaluation process, organizations should create two new categories of which to base employee performance, as suggested by Johnson et al. (2009, p. 409) and Li and Hung (2009).

The first category should involve core task requirements: Those tasks prescribed and recognized as part of a particular job and are reviewed and weighted as 75% of the performance evaluation. The second category should involve OCB requirements, the informal, pro-social acts benefitting co-workers, supervisors, and the organization, which are reviewed and weighted as 25% of the performance evaluation. Following the implementation of the new processes leaders should research the impact of fairness perceptions as it relates to: a) organizational effectiveness, b) gender, c) results-based versus production based-performance, d) procedural justice, the employee influence in decision-making based on consistent and unbiased processes, and e) interactional justice, the interpersonal treatment during evaluation process (Fournier, 2008). The final step would be for leaders to determine the impact of transformational leadership theory on employee motivation to exhibit OCB.

According to Chiaburu, Oh, Berry, Li, and Gardner (2011) the literature indicated a need to recognize and combine several theories of human resources performance practices, relationships between organizations, human resources, leaders, and employees. More in-depth research is needed to define specific roles and relationships among these groups, and then to develop an action plan or model to implement the theories and practices into the organizations. The successful research, creation, and

implementation of a new model may provide human
resources managers the opportunity to demonstrate
its ability to contribute to the success of the
organization and the individual employees.

**Title Searches, Articles, Research Documents,
and Journals.**

Multiple databases, such as ProQuest
Dissertations and Theses, EbscoHost, Emerald, and
the Education Resources Information Center were
accessed for published and unpublished literature to
prevent publishing bias (Cooper & Schindler, 2002).
The focus of key words in searches were the topics of
organizational citizenship behavior. Through the
online title search for organizational citizenship
behaviors and other important keywords including:
organizational citizenship behavior, social exchange
theory, organizational behavior, human resources
management, leadership theory, performance
reviews, fairness, and interactional justice, several
peer-reviewed books and journal articles were easily
accessible. The variety of research information
available in brick-and-mortar libraries and on the

Internet was conducive to successful access to research documents. The literature search resulted in the compilation of approximately 175 published articles, dissertations, and books.

History and Definition of Organizational Citizenship Behavior.

Dennis Organ is the pioneer of organizational citizenship behavior he linked quickly to the social exchange theory developed by Emerson (1976). Organ (1977) completed research on the subject through the published dissertation, *A Reappraisal and Reinterpretation of the Satisfaction-Causes-Performance Hypothesis,* where the emphasis on employee satisfaction causes increased performance. The underlying concept in Organ's dissertation (1977) hypothesized that employees expect recognition for a job well done, and was supported; however, to what extreme employees held that expectation was not identified. Through further collaborative research by Organ and his students, the concept of OCB became increasingly interesting in organizational processes. Smith et al. (1983) defined organizational citizenship behavior (OCB) as individual mood, actions, and reactions influenced by the ability to be autonomous.

Organizational citizenship behaviors are linked to task interdependence, meaning that individuals incorporate OCB into performing ordinary and daily tasks; partially through the additional intrinsic exhibition of altruism and extroversion (Smith et al., 1983). Historically, management has created an atmosphere of negativity and cultural chaos where employees concentrated solely on pre-determined individual accomplishments and goals toward attaining organizational goals. According to Organ (1977) part of the reason for the lack of ability to define clearly how and when OCB is occurring in organizations is the many variations of OCB, which at the time had not been considered for research. Over the past 40 years the concept of OCB has been intermittently researched, but more so over the past 10 years.

The individual framework of OCB by Kreitner (2004) embraced the concept of an '*I and me*' perspective of employees. This cultural concept is based on individualistic achievements and goals. In contrast, the concept of '*us and we*' is used in other

Eastern countries, such as Japan (Emerson, 1976), a country that eschews individualism and embraces teams and groups. When Dr. W. Edwards Deming went to Japan to work on his concept of Total Quality Management (TQM), he used the cultural model of Japan, where the benefit to many people outweighs the benefit to only one person (Kreitner, 2004) where OCB is exhibited individually to benefit everyone. Organizations can learn from Deming's contributions to the cultural concept of organizational relationship building by recognizing the contributions of OCB as part of individual and team-related performance (Feldman, 1996).

Davis (1996) supported the need to recognize employee contributions through organizational design and culture, specifically in authoritarian organizations. Davis (1996) and Collins (1997) suggested leaders needed to perform an end-means analysis to determine the rules, roles, norms, and values that must occur to build stable individual and team relationships. By using organizational theory leaders succeeded in building trust, and cooperation for a strong organizational culture. Organizational theory is grounded in authoritarianism and is justified because both are essential for achieving very specific strategic design goals. Organizational values are basic, fundamental, enduring, absolute, and irrevocable. Organizational values are taken *literally* and acted on (Giblin & Amuso, 1997).

Organizational behavior theory (OB) is a field of study that investigates the impact that individuals, groups, and organizational structure have on behavior within organizations and applying such knowledge toward improving an organization's effectiveness (Brown, 2011; Summers et al., 1997). In moving OB forward, Hesselbein, Goldsmith, and Beckhard (1997) uncovered several organizational practices and

theories where OCB may be practiced. Organizations
rely on outsourcing, such as multi-national and trans-
national operations. Ozen and Kusku, 2009)
suggested a need to recognize shifts in organizational
theory and structure. The shifts and changes must
reflect the contributions of employees of OCBs to
become a "New Organization" (Hesselbein et al.,
1997, p. 5). Employee contributions build on Chiu and
Tsai's (2006) definition of OCB: "Extra-role behavior
that is not directly, explicitly, and formally rewarded by
the organization" (p. 518). Emotional burnout and
exhaustion have a negative effect on employees and
therefore on the organization and results in a
decrease of OCB. Jha and Jha (2009) determined
that sensitivities toward individual, group, and
organizational success influenced the extent to which
employees exhibited OCB, and a lack of recognition
exacerbated the negative effects.

Hesselbein et al. (1997) also brought to light
effective commitment because of intrinsic motivation
as researched by Kuvaas (2007; 2008) who states
positive feedback is also a motivator for growth and
growth measurement. Kinicki and Kreitner (2006), in
agreement with Kuvaas (2007; 2008), suggested pay-

for-performance is relative to employee work performance and effective commitment. Kuvaas (2007; 2998) studied ways that organizations motivated and influenced the work performance of employees and how leadership motivation and influence relate to the exhibition of OCB in helping employees meet strategic organizational goals and increase job satisfaction. The exchange relationship between the leader and employee is significant regarding work value, performance, and turnover, influencing positive or negative attitudes (Shore, Tetrick, Lynch, & Barksdale, 2006). Colbert and Wiit (2007) examined the exchange relationships and noted a definite increase in altruism.

Altruism influences positive and effective employee performance using motivational leadership to extract the behaviors to achieve specific performance goals (Colbert & Wiit, 2007). Sun et al. (2007) determined challenges exist in determining valid measures of successful contributions of OCB, documenting the positive relationships between high-performance human resources and organizational performance. Unfortunately, the employee perceptions of fairness in the rewards and recognition

of job performance have not been or defined
(Fournier, 2008).

Research by Chen et al. (2009) and Organ
(1977) defined OCB as "individual behavior that is
discretionary" (p. 47). The specific behaviors of OCB
include altruism, conscientiousness, sportsmanship,
courtesy, and civic virtue (Chen, et al., 2009; Organ,
1977). OCB is also highly correlated with high-
commitment and high-performance employees, such
as those in the service and hospitality industries.
Chen, et al. (2009) discuss the need for job
standardization to enable organizations to narrow the
gap of performance inequality perceptions of
employees.

According to Chen et al. (2009) organizations
categorize OCB by extra-role and in-role activities
(Organ, 1977) that separate the personal objectives
from organizational objectives. Chen et al. (2009, p.
45) recognized altruism and courtesy as important
personal values and objectives exhibited by
employees and that organizational leaders take for
granted. Altruism and courtesy are categorized as
organizational citizenship behaviors intrinsic to
individuals (OCB-I), whereas the organization benefits

from employees who exhibit sportsmanship, civic virtue, and conscientiousness therefore OCB is categorized as organizational citizenship behaviors expected as a member of the organization (OCB-O) (Chen et al., 2009, p. 45).

Leadership Theories.

Social exchange theory dates to the 1950s and continues to develop as scholars review literature and gather data. Emerson (1976) cites the work of several pioneers of social exchange theory (Homans, 1958, 1961, 1974; Thibaut & Kelley, 1959; Blau, 1964) – with Blau (1964) forging the way for future scholars. "Social exchange ... is limited to actions that are contingent on rewarding reactions from others" (Emerson, 1976, p. 336) and is parallel to structural functionalism. Another phrase provided by Emerson (1976) for social exchange theory is "strategic interaction" (p. 336). Regardless of the definition of social exchange theory, the meaning and action are still unchanged; almost quid pro quo. An employee performs an act that benefits others, including the organization, and receives something in return. The question of what the employee receives in return is still unclear and may continue to be unclear unless organizations recognize a need for change, design, and implement an action plan.

Azuka (2009) stated "A test of a true leader is his capacity to adhere to a strong foundation of ethics, articulate them as standards for colleagues and staff, and practice what he preaches by example on a daily basis" (p. 11). Borial, Caer, and Baron (2009) discussed environmental leadership practices citing the seven principal action logics of Rooke and Torbert (2005): Opportunist, diplomat, expert, achiever, individualist, strategist, and alchemist, and how each affected environmental leadership. In this capacity, managers did the leading and employees did what they were told to do.

As leadership practices evolved, participative management theories became part of the political, social, and philosophical assumptions in applying various leadership techniques, including organizational design management practices (Von Aken, 2007). New leadership used participatory management to show management and democracy share many social philosophical assumptions in organizational leadership practices (Collins, 1997). One such assumption is employees have an equal share in the success or failure of an organization. Using participative management increased over the past 10 years, but not exclusively. Organizational leaders are as independent and individualistic as any other member of the organization, as are leadership theories to individual leaders.

Leader's task orientation is important at the outset and creates changes to relationship orientation, as a project moves toward a goal the leader becomes a model (Kivlighan, 1997). Kivlighan

(1997) suggested some organizational events require the use of situational leadership theory. Part of leadership responsibilities are to determine how the need for task and relationship transformations are perceived by other leaders, and to lead the events as required from one situation to another. Kivlighan (1997) also stated transformational leadership uses a situational theory design. As the organization transforms and new situations arise, leadership must make use of a collection of management tools for shaping tomorrow's organizations (Hesselbein et al., 1997).

Transformational leaders as defined by Yukl (1999) recognize the strengths and weaknesses of transformational and charismatic leadership theories besides other conceptual leadership theories. The recognition of the need to enable employees to be the most productive falls under research by Judge and Bono (2000) who discussed the *Five Factor Model of Personality/Transformational Leadership Extroversion and Agreeableness* predicted in transformational leadership. The characteristics of transformational leadership behaviors are reflected in the effectiveness and control of organizational goals and strategies, including managing and leading people. Jha and Jha (2009) also reported transformational leadership behaviors influenced and stimulated the exhibition of extroverted behaviors from employees.

Monroe, Hankin, and Van Vechten (2000) discussed social psychology, cognition, roles, and social construction. As part of intergroup relations, social dominance, and realistic group conflict, employees perceived leadership roles and responsibilities as directly affecting the performance and production in the organization. Management is not an exact science, but is a mix of art, scientific methods, intuition, investigation, and experimentation (Miller, 2001, p. 11). Motivational and transformational leadership have been an effective mechanism by which charismatic leaders create positive emotional experiences in followers through effective use of positive personality traits (Ilies, Judge, & Wagner, 2006). The positive emotional experiences are cognitive mechanisms induced by the communication of a leader's vision of goal setting and is connected via charismatic and transformational leadership influencing employee motivation.

Cunliffe (2008) provided information regarding the social constructionist theory where personal experiences are shaped by social interactions. Leaders and followers enjoin in communication through words, art, and gestures offering humans the ability to interpret meanings and events from an internal perspective (p. 124). Later Cunliffe (2009) added the theory of relationships and the teaching perspective of leadership. The perspective that leaders lead and followers follow only holds true for a short period; the follower becomes the leader and teacher for peers – and possibly other leaders.

Keeffee, Darling, and Natesan (2008) discussed the use of 360 management and leadership and performance reviews. Effective leadership teams require a diverse group of individuals with varying talents and knowledge (SMEs) in the most important organizational areas: research and development, accounting, finance, human resources, logistics, marketing, and production (Keeffee et al., 2008). These talents enhance others and create a paradigm for an integrated cross-functional operational design (p. 90). Besides the new paradigm, Dreachslin and Hobby (2008) discussed

diversity in leadership where organizational behaviors
exhibited by leaders and employees have a direct
positive or negative effect on the outcomes of health
issues. These social factors must be reviewed and
changed.

Baeza, Lao, Meneses, and Roma (2009)
discussed charismatic leadership. The emergence of
effective climate at the team level results directly from
charismatic leadership – based on followers'
perceptions of a leader's behavior in a positive light.
The discussion evaluated the impact of charismatic
leadership behaviors on cooperation, tension, and
motivation (p. 515). Hickman (2010) added
charismatic and transformational leadership has a
direct influence on employees exhibiting
organizational citizenship behaviors and the
perception of developing shared decision-making
powers with leaders (p. 567).

Behavioral Management Theories.

Mayer and Russell (1987) stated social
behavior modeling may be an effective management
tool in organizations. A group of scientists were

placed in a negative, uncomfortable, and stressful situation for an extended time. The discussion by Leon, Kanfer, Hoffman, and Dupre (1994) related the outcome of close work proximity and lack of leadership guidance in this situation. The results of the social behavior modeling and social environment studies showed a link between negative (inactivity or nonperformance) and positive behaviors (compliance and altruism). Podsakoff et al. (2009) agreed social behaviors affect organizational behaviors and major positive and negative consequences of OCB exist.

Brink (2001) discussed organizational corporate culture theory where cultures have been given names, such as "power, role, task and persons orientations; rational, hierarchical, ideological, and consensual" (p. 39). Color-coding used Porter's Typology and Organizational Aspects: cool green, hot red, true blue, and a dull gray. Diagnoses of which color or typology reflects the culture of the organization can assist with recognition for a need for change. Kegan and Laley (2009) discuss ways to influence and embrace change within organizations through embracing organizational cultural change. Organizational culture was a major factor in creating environmental leadership theories. Leaders must adapt their strategies and management practices to address the environmental challenges to foster sustainable cultural development of the organization. Adaptive leadership required the dissemination of environmental factors in leadership (Borial et al., (2009). Another environmental factor of organizational change is the emotional intelligence exhibited by employees (Schoo, 2008; Wang & Huang, 2009).

Emotional intelligence as defined by Yaghoubi, Mashinchi, and Hadi (2011) is the ability to control individual emotions, and to understand others effectively, and direct others in a positive manner. Yaghoubi et al. determined that OCB has been widely used in previous studies, such as research by Walz and Niehoff (1996), and OCB has been found to affect organizational effectiveness. The research study revealed a correlation between leadership exhibition of emotional intelligence and employee exhibition OCB. The most notable correlation was between the heightened exhibition of conscientiousness and altruism, building trust, and strengthening organizational culture.

Employee Culture.

Thompson (2008) provided a personal
leadership view of corporate culture when leading
organizational change with a group of employees and
the path taken to increase leader/follower trust.
Stating that culture is a necessary factor in shaping
organizational relationships, Schein (1996) included
trust in a study of management theory and
organizational leadership. Schien (1990) stated the
content of organizational cultures is the byproduct of
the internal and external effects of human behaviors
and social psychology behaviors. In his study, Schein
(1996) explained diverse behaviors affected the
relationships between leaders and followers, and
shaped the organizational culture.

Organizational cultures are created by perceptions and contributions of employees and the relationships between employees (Holt, Bjorklund, & Green, 2009). Something of note, regarding organizational cultures, is the incorporation of commonly shared individual morals and standards that can be integrated into the organizational culture (Spitzeck, 2009). A side-effect of shaping organizational cultures included many organizational transformations. Hesselbein et al. (1997) discussed organizational transformation as several organizational practices and theories, to include outsourcing, multi-national operations, trans-national operations, shifts in theory and structure, and the contributions of employees to move toward "New Organizations" (p. 5), or learning organizations.

Pavlica, Holman, and Thorpe (1998) suggested using social constructionist perspectives, such as managers working toward becoming a *practical author* or learning and leading the "process of learning" (p. 300) to stimulate thinking about managers as leaders and teachers. Some of the ways learning can be stimulated include:

- Formal recognition of organizational citizenship behaviors (OCBs) by implementing several organizational practices and theories, including shifts in theory and structure, and the contributions of employees, to move toward becoming a learning culture.

- Increase developmental feedback through dissemination of a well written organizational values statement, adapted to define the core business purpose and crucial to competitive success (Giblin & Amuso, 1997).

- Including performance measurements based on a basic to list, measuring communication and the relevancy to individual contributions and high performance teams (Chiocchio, 2007).

- Understanding how interactional justice works within the organization. Interactional justice is the expectation of how power and influence create emotional reactions (Fournier, 2008), and employee perceptions of fairness within the supervisor/subordinate relationship (Willer et al., 1997).

- Questioning why employees go above and beyond the call of duty in work performance (Good Citizen Syndrome) defined by Willer et al. (1997) and how pro-social motivation enhances persistence, performance, and productivity (Grant, 2008).

- Understanding the significance of altruism, influenced by individual mood, actions, reactions, the ability to be spontaneous, extroversion, and task interdependence (Smith et al., 1983).

- Understanding organizational behaviors, a field of study that investigates the impact individuals, groups, and structure have on behavior within organizations to apply such knowledge toward improving an organization's effectiveness (Summers et al., 1997, p. 347).

- Discussing how positive and negative moods exhibited during job performance is treated as isolated moods in relation to employee creativity and affects individual and group performance jointly (George, 2007).

Considering the investigation of
employee/employer relationships, Sun et al.
researched the patterns and relationships conducive
to organizational performance and learning. By
examining the behaviors of employees, human
resources leaders developed high quality practices for
sustaining relationships, recruiting and retaining
knowledgeable employees (Sun et al., 2007, p. 559).
Tying OCB to "high quality, open-ended relationships
and learning" (Sun et al., 2007, p. 559) indicates a
long-term relationship and investment in employees.
Once employees and leaders become comfortable in
their relationships, loyalty, and contributory role
behaviors become reciprocated, the interdependency
and mutuality of the relationships between leaders
and employees increased (Sun et al., 2007, p. 560).

The main hypotheses Sun et al. supported are
that high-performance practices are positively related
to service-oriented OCB; OCB mediates the
relationship between high-performance human
resources practices and turnover; service-oriented
OCB mediates the relationship between high-
performance human resources practices and
productivity. In high-performance organizations the

unemployment rate moderates the service-oriented OCB-turnover relationship so the relationship is stronger when unemployment rates are low rather than when they are high. The business strategy moderates the service-oriented OCB-productivity relationship so the relationship is stronger for organizations with service-quality strategy rather than a low-cost strategy (Sun et al., 2007, p. 561).

The hypotheses provided by Sun et al. (2007) were supported with the exception the unemployment rate moderates the service-oriented OCB-turnover relationship so the relationship is stronger when unemployment rates are lower than when they are high; this was false (Sun et al., 2007). The results of Sun et al. (2007) research upholds the argument that implementing high-performance human resources practices is conducive to increasing service-oriented practices through mediating organizational citizenship behaviors.

Human Resources Management.

The importance of human capital to
organizations in the past century has changed. In the
early part of the 1900s employees were treated like
extended family, often spoken to as one would speak
to a brother or sister, and included in personal
functions by managers or business owners. In the
second half of the 1900s, human resources
processes changed. Where the human resources
division was only a department that processes
recruiting, hiring, payroll, and termination of
employees in the early 1900s, organizational leaders
were inspired to integrate human resources practices
to organizational strategy (Legnick-Hall & Legnick-
Hall, 1988). Once this change was made, the
emergence of the more flexible organization became
the norm where the strategies presented and
designed by leaders became known as Strategic
Human Resources Management (SHRM) (not to be
confused with the trade organization with the same
acronym).

Strategic Human Resources Management (SHRM) functions and strategies are used in various disciplines within organizations. A study by Ferris, Hochwarter, Buckley, Harrell-Cook, and Frink (1999) adopted a cross-functional approach of training, compensation, and performance appraisal. The research by Ferris et al. (1999, p. 1070) hypothesized that organizations sustained competitive advantage through High-Performance Work Systems (HPWS) and depended on the level and performance of collective human capital. In the discovery process discussed by Ferris et al. and in a recent study by Takeuchi, Lepak, Wang, and Takeuchi (2007), the use of HPWS is positively related to a high degree of social exchange within an organization. Introducing the HPWS in organizations influenced the addition of training and development of KSAs to assist employees in acting in a socially acceptable manner in the workplace (Ferris, 1999).

Cohn, Katzenbach, and Vlak (2008) stated that finding and developing innovative talent through mentoring and peer networks would increase individual and group innovation. As employee innovation increased, so did the exhibition of OCB. If recognized as part of the necessary KSAs, an increase in performance and production would be noted. Chiaburu, Oh, Berry, Li, and Gardner (2011) stated: "Although organizations typically select employees for their ability to reach requisite levels of task performance, research indicates that citizenship is important for organizational success" (p. 1150).

Organizations that train and develop HPWS will use successful innovators to groom the next generations of innovators. Employee participation in mentoring and coaching other employees positively affected job satisfaction. Rowold (2008) suggested the best way to foster continual growth of employee innovation and growth organizations design and implement HR development interventions with a positive effect on KSAs through technical and non-technical training. Snape and Redmond (2010) concluded human resources management practices positively affect organizational citizenship participation by employees, regardless of organizational support and commitment. Part of the social exchange value of the nontechnical training is the use of stories and experience to stimulate innovative dialogue and idea sharing among employees. As employees become comfortable with this training, they will use the new knowledge to perform job tasks, positively affecting employee satisfaction and innovation.

Jana (2009) stated, "Change is inevitable, growth is intentional," which was a symposium topic in 2005. Innovation brings about organizational changes, including cultural and procedural changes. The employee performance review process is formulated to measure the level of success or failure of employees to perform the tasks assigned when the organization hires the employees. Organizations have measures of behaviors required by employees. These behaviors are not always the values and norms with a direct effect on the achievement of individuals, teams, and the organization (Jones, 2004). Cultural values are an important reference point for establishing relationships and organizational commitment (Jones, 2004).

Leadership behavior has a positive impact on development of team cohesion and influences superior performance (Michalisin, Karau, & Tangpong, 2007). Dysvik and Kuvaas (2008) studied the employee and leadership behaviors and discovered the best practice perspective is superior organizational performance is achieved when employees exert energy on behalf of the organization ... fulfilling employee needs and generating favorable attitudes and behaviors resulting in increased performance (p. 2). The perception of employee obligation increases employee motivation to work hard for the organization (Dysvik & Kuvaas, 2008, p. 2).

Performance Reviews.

Fiol, Pratt, and O'Conner (2009) discussed the identity conflicts within organizations because most performance reviews do not include employee contributions toward individual and organizational goals. Moseley and Dessinger (2010) suggested methods of measuring employee and organizational performance and ways to improve performance. First, organizations have an opportunity to use various leadership tools to increase employee retention, productivity, altruism, and satisfaction while providing recognition and rewards. Most employees are satisfied with verbal recognition, such as spontaneous words of appreciation (thank you), but expect a monetary or other form of remuneration for excellent job performance (Rosen et al., 1991). Employee rewards and benefits processes are part of organizational human resources management through behavioral incentives that provide compensation. Swanson (1999) argued performance improvement strategies contributed to organizational success, reducing turnover through the recognition of diversity and personal relationships. High-performance employees who exhibit OCBs increase the sustainability and functionality of organizations and expect to receive additional benefits and compensation for such performance (Nishii & Mayer, 2009).

The best way to gain value from human capital is to understand the underlying psychological dynamics of people: to provide them meaning, understanding, and education (Swanson, 1999, p. 15). Psychological theory is based on "purposive behavior" (Swanson, 1999, p. 15) effectively focusing on the behavioral and cognitive processes and goals of individuals within the organization to include OCB. Employee behaviors, such as motivation, information processing, and group dynamics, play a major role in successfully using cognitive theory. Swanson (1999) states the goals and ideas of individuals become part of the organizational strategies – a way to create employee buy-in toward results for the organization (p. 21). These behaviors may stimulate employee OCB.

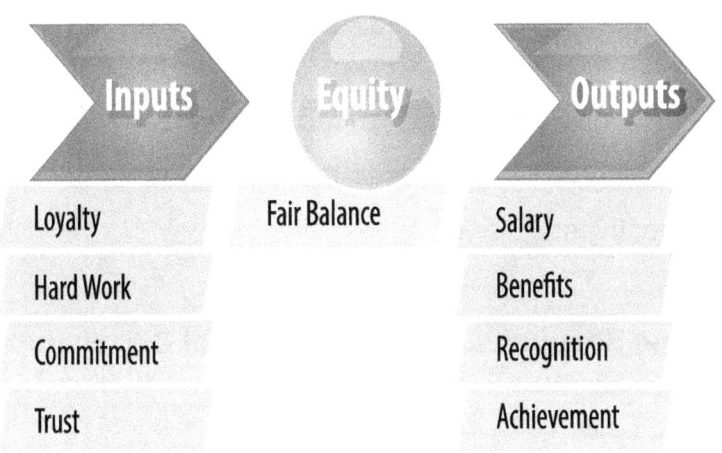

Loyalty

Hard Work

Commitment

Trust

Fair Balance

Salary

Benefits

Recognition

Achievement

Systems theory connects the inputs, outputs, changes, future needs, and feedback to the mission, vision, and strategy of the organization through general, chaos, and futures theory (Swanson, 1999). The chaos theory relates directly to the meaning of the word *chaos*: upheaval and constant change, something inevitable, but the only true constant in organizations. How organizations focus on the "process of becoming and not being" (Swanson, 1999, p. 18) in the constant motion of change depends on the futures theory, or forecasting and planning for the future because of the chaos (Richards, 2008). In these chaotic processes, the balance of employee wants with employee needs becomes a major dilemma that fuels the conflict between the desire to perform well or not to perform well (Rowe, 2009). A lack of recognition for performing well only adds to the chaos from employee perspectives.

Formal Recognition of Organizational Citizenship Behaviors.

No prior proof or research exists that OCB is formally recognized in the performance review process. Scott and Davis (2007, p. 151) stated the recognition of behaviors determines and defines the extent to which employees believe they are members of an organization. Several organizational practices, such as shifts in leadership, behavioral theories, organizational structure, and the recognition of

specific individual contributions of employees can
assist in transforming organizations toward becoming
"New Organizations" (Hesselbein et al., 1997, p. 5).
As part of a new organizational shift in recognizing
employee contributions, Schmidt (2007) stated
employees who believe they are important members
of organizations through the training and development
they receive as part of their job performance are more
satisfied and, in turn, are more productive for the
organization. Li, Liang, and Crant (2010) uncovered
proof employees relate OCBs to individual job
success and satisfaction.

Goal Setting and Organizational Staffing.

Employee performance and behaviors are
based on several behavioral models affecting
organizational goals. These behavioral models affect
specific jobs should be staffed and play a major part
in the performance and attainment of organizational
goals. Galbraith (1974, p. 28) examined two specific
behavioral models: the information processing model,
and the mechanistic behavioral model. The
information processing model stated the greater the

task uncertainty, the greater the amount of information that must be processed among decision makers during task execution to achieve a given level of performance. The mechanistic model stated the behaviors that occur in one sub-task cannot be judged as good or bad; the behaviors are effective or ineffective, depending on the behaviors of the subtask performers (Galbraith, 1974, p. 28). Therefore, the structure of an organization depends on its behavioral environments and a congruence (or match) between environments, structures, and behaviors leads to high organizational performance (Randolph & Dess, 1984).

Teamwork.

According to research by Allen (2009), teamwork is a shared purpose, culture, and foundation of conduct in which employees feel comfortable and committed toward organizational goals. The successful performance of individual roles and responsibilities becomes the catalyst for team accomplishments. Accomplishments of individuals are also measured by the success of collaborative efforts among employees (Allen, 2009). Organizational performance measures include the ability of employees to perform in collaborative teams with or without leadership. The level of innovation in any organizational culture defines the internal and external effects of human behavior and social psychology behaviors (Zhang, Hempel, Han, & Tjosvold, 2007). Schein (1996) discussed how social behaviors affect the relationships between leaders and followers and cultivated the emergence of team cognition and performance. Team cognition emerges through interactions of team members and in effect distinguishes high-performing teams from other kinds of teams (Cooke, Gorman, Duran, & Taylor, 2007). High performing employees are part of a team culture where individuals exhibit OCBs. Recognition of quality, discipline, delegation, team spirit, and communication by leaders transfers into training, encouragement, motivation, coaching, praise, recognition, rewards, and positive performance feedback (Andolsen, 2008). Carson, Tesluk, and Marrone (2007, p. 1219) also stated that the influence of leadership recognition enabled a higher level of team and organizational performance.

Innovation.

High-performing employees are a sign of the
strength and effectiveness of organizational leaders,
exhibiting the adaptability of the organization to meet
short-term priorities and long-term strategies (Bonini,
Koller, & Mirvis, 2009). High-performance teams and
individuals are motivated by the ability to be
innovative and creative (Maital & Seshadri, 2007).
According to an organizational culture index provided
by Wallach (1983, p. 733) as cited by Maital and
Seshadri (2007), organizations that placed the right
individuals in the right jobs discovered an increase in
employee innovation. The conclusion of the study is
employees are only likely to be innovative and
creative in their jobs if they are satisfied with the work
and performing the organization (Lee & Chang, 2008).
Satisfied employees provided organizations the
opportunity to identify and groom innovators,
increasing the excellence of organizational talent.
Cohn et al. (2008) determined that organizations that
enabled mentoring and peer networks increased
innovation and creativity, and a network of successful
innovators to groom the next generation of innovators.

Relationship Building.

Research showed positive feedback enhanced
leadership belief in employee self-efficacy (Chiocchio,
2007, p. 106). Leaders are in a position of power and
influence on relationships (Bowen & Inkpen, 2009).
Michalsin et al. (2007) stated "leadership has the
potential to operate as an intangible strategic asset"
(p. 2) for the organization and had a dramatic effect
on team cohesion and relationship building.
Employees satisfied with relationships they have with
other employees and leaders are more satisfied and,
in turn, are more productive for the organization
(Schmidt, 2007). Strong relationships provide an
arena for constructive feedback, recognition, and
rewards contributing to the strengths and weaknesses
(individual and as a team) within organizations Parker
(2008).

Recognition and Rewards.

Culbert (2010) deconstructed the performance
review process and stated the employee perception of
recognition and rewards is negative. The base

premise of most employees was leaders did not
recognize individual contributions as OCB, nor did
employees receive recognition and rewards based on
OCB. Culbert (2010) suggested organizations stop
using the performance review as the process is
detrimental to motivation and negatively influences
employee performance and satisfaction. Rosen et al.
(1991) argued many management and behavior
incentives, such as pay-for-performance without
review, are negatively received by employees.
Buntzman and Parker (2008) discussed the
leadership perspective of providing recognition and
rewards for employee performance reviews.

From a leadership perspective the research
concluded recognition and rewards do not influence
employee perceptions of employee value to the
organization (Buntzman & Parker, 2008). Employees'
perceptions indicate recognition and rewards improve
the clarity of performing to the benefit of attaining the
organizational mission and values. With this
extremely opposite perspective of recognition and
rewards, positive views and actions by leadership
equals positive employee perceptions; the converse is
present for negativity (Buntzman & Parker, 2008, p.

82). Podsakoff et al. (2009) discussed the inclusion of counterproductive work habits as part of employee performance reviews that noticeably hindered an increase in employee performance and satisfaction. The conclusions of Podsakoff et al. (2009) are refuted by Spector, Bauer, and Fox (2010): counterproductive behaviors and OCBs were found to be unrelated (p. 781). Buntzman and Parker's (2008) conclusion of the employee perspective is negative feedback or lack of recognition and rewards can affect the job retention, satisfaction, and performance.

Chen and Chiu (2009) conclude employee perceptions affect job characteristics and OCB are based on five core job dimensions defined by Hackman and Oldham (1975, p. 476):

- Skill variety – the extent employees use different skills
- Task identity – the extent to which employees can complete work
- Task significance – the substantive effect the performance of the job has on others
- Autonomy – employees' sense of independence and the discretion to work at own pace

- Feedback- information received from performance reviews, supervisors, peers, and customers

In the study by Chen and Klimoski (2007), job roles are a mediating factor in the relationship between job characteristics and OCB. Participants in the study by Chen and Klimoski (2007) indicated the perception of a specific unspoken contractual responsibility to exhibit OCB while performing job tasks. Employee perceptions are important to job satisfaction. According to Chen and Chiu (2009) positive employee perceptions of a job well done, or going above and beyond, derive from internal motivation to continue to excel in job performance. Besides increased employee job satisfaction, OCB is closely associated with employee perceptions of personal satisfaction in job performance (Chen & Chiu, 2009). Chen and Chiu (2009) determined by standardizing job tasks, organizations might increase OCB, thereby increasing employee and organizational efficiency.

A gap exists between leaders watching the bottom line for the organization rather than the results of output and production by employee contributions to the strategic goals of the organization. Organizations fail to include the strategic human resources planning (SHRP) functions in the organizational growth agenda, to include design and culture of innovative work systems, and provide or sustain recognition and reward processes (Laurie & Lynch, 2007, p. 27). The design of strategic human resources planning activities must fit the competitive environment, best practices, hiring, training, compensation, recognition, and rewards, to include performance-based compensation (Khilji & Wang, 2006, p. 1172). Several complementary human resources practices act to influence the same organizational goals, but bundling human resources practices with organizational strategy can influence positively employee and organizational performance, (e.g., positivity affects commitment, skill levels, use of experience, employee satisfaction) (Toh, Morgeson, & Campion, 2008). The implication to leaders is the alignment of strategic goals must include processes that influence employee performance toward the attainment of organizational goals; the inclusion of human resources planning is essential (Sitzmann, Brown, Casper, Ely, & Zimmerman, 2008).

Chen et al. (2009, as cited by Organ, 1977) defined organizational citizenship behaviors (OCB) as "individual behavior that is discretionary" (p. 39) and not part of the formal job performance evaluation and recognition process of the organization. Organizational leaders lack a formal process to recognize and reward the value-added by employees who exhibit OCBs. This lack of recognition in performance evaluations by leaders appears to affect the productivity of employees who exhibit OCB. The traditional behaviors of generic job descriptions do not provide the recognition for those behaviors exhibited by employees over and above the behaviors officially defined when an employee is hired (Kinicki & Kreitner, 2006). The lack of recognition for behaviors not traditionally recognized may affect employees desire to be productive, or work as part of a team, and include general job task performance, professional, and personal job satisfaction (Allen, 2009). The research study answered the research question and determined the accuracy of the hypothesis:

Q[1]: What effect will leadership recognition of OCBs in performance evaluations in Washington State healthcare organizations have on employees' productivity, teamwork, job performance, and satisfaction?

H[1]: There is an increase in productivity, teamwork, job performance, and satisfaction because of implementing a formal process of recognizing and rewarding employees for exhibiting OCB as part of the employee evaluation process.

H[0]: There is no increase in productivity, teamwork, job performance, and satisfaction because of implementing a formal process of recognizing and rewarding employees for exhibiting OCB as part of the employee evaluation process.

Von Bertalanffy (1972) performed a quantitative analysis regarding the changing paradigm of how social groups perceive, process, and resolve complex phenomena. The study discussed specific methods of investigation derived from general

systems theory called "organismic biology" (p. 410),
where the perceptions of individuals influence
personal and group-related motivation, satisfaction,
and performance (Von Bertalanffy, 1972). A lack of
motivation, job satisfaction, and leadership
recognition for a job well done has an emotional and
financial cost to organizations. A secondary objective
of the study is to determine if implementing the formal
recognition of OCB as part of the employee
evaluation process is a cost-effective measure to
increase employee productivity, teamwork, and job
satisfaction in healthcare organizations in Washington
State. The objective is to ensure the research
considers the various areas of leadership and cultural
influence while staying within the specific direction
proposed in the problem statement (Cooper &
Schindler, 2002).

Conclusion

The literature reflects a need for leaders to
reward and recognize the exhibition of OCB within
organizations (Chen & Chiu, 2009, Sun et al., 2007).
Understanding and using the management theories

through the decades of literature is the key to moving forward toward incorporating OCB into a performance review process. Recognizing employee contributions over and above the generic job tasks may enable organizations to add to the stability of employee retention, which results directly from increased employee job satisfaction and trust in leadership (Chen et al., 2009). Developing leadership-training programs regarding the recognition of OCBs exhibited by employees is a key element for the human resources department. By providing leaders the tools to build relationships with employees and the tools to assist with implementing the recognition of OCB in the formal performance review process organizations may realize an increase in productivity, employee retention, and job satisfaction.

Training by the human resources department is important to affecting organizational change, leader and employee expectations are important to the development of any organizational design change. Employees expect pay-for-performance and to be paid for their time, knowledge, education, training, and other tasks performed through leadership delegation. Research by Johnson et al. (2009) states employees have an expectation that every task they perform is part of the performance review and evaluation process, including OCB behaviors. Human resources practices enable leaders to enjoy job standardization and lack the ability for leaders to recognize OCBs exhibited by employees. A lack of flexibility in job performance and employees' recognition of OCB performance may have a direct effect on employee's performance, satisfaction, retention, and ability to work within a team.

Organizational design and culture also have a direct effect on the recognition of OCB in organizations. Designing employee performance parameters to create a fair and equitable set of employee roles and responsibilities may increase the exhibition of OCB. The recognition of OCBs as part of the performance evaluation process will assist in creating an additional set of values within the organizational culture (Chen, et al., 2009) increasing the results-based view for employees and performance and results-based information for leaders. The only way to attain these goals is for organizations to complete an internal analysis to determine if a benefit exists by formally recognizing employees who exhibit OCB as part of the formal performance evaluation process in Washington State healthcare organizations.

Summary

The research of Chen and Chiu (2009) provided a definite link between mood, altruism, motivation, and the perceived value, appreciation, and fairness of rewards and recognition of employees who may exhibit OCB. The organizational design and how it affects the creation and supports the organizational culture has a direct effect on the roles, norms, and values employees embrace (Chen & Chiu, 2009). Further research may determine the value to organizations that recognize and reward employees who exhibit OCB. The literature review suggested certain leadership styles may influence employee exhibition of OCB over others. The literature also suggested leader-follower relationships affected the commitment of employees' opportunities or motives to exhibit OCB and whether leaders recognized or rewarded OCB. Chapter three provided information regarding the research design, data collection

process, data analysis, and a research design with
the intentions of determining whether organizations
may benefit from leadership recognition and inclusion
of OCB in formal job performance evaluations.

CHAPTER III
METHODS AND PROCEDURES

The purpose of this descriptive, quantitative study was to analyze the benefit of formally recognizing employees who exhibit OCB as part of the formal performance evaluation process. A random sample of 115 employees representing each of 10 various healthcare industries in Washington State, to include employees holding management and non-management positions determined leadership recognition of OCB positively affects employee productivity, teamwork, job satisfaction, and rewards. The important elements of the descriptive, quantitative research design was the research method, data collection, data instrument, informed consent, confidentiality, data analysis, validity, and reliability. Neuman (2003) suggested researchers must decide what results to expect at the conclusion of a study based on quantitative or qualitative. The choice of performing a quantitative versus a qualitative research design provided results based on statistical calculations.

The research discussion answered the question of why one method is most appropriate over others and determined if any positive benefits exist. The proper research design is essential. The data collection method and instrument affected the decision on which research method to use and was appropriate to answer the research question. The research discussion also addressed the method and processes for obtaining informed consent and protected the confidentiality of the participants. An overview of the data analysis method, appropriateness, validity, and reliability of the research provided information regarding the data collection as part of the final discussion and dissemination of the data.

Research Method and Design Appropriateness

The elements of the selected design were descriptive and quantitative because the majority of available literature relevant to the subject of OCB was also quantitative. Employee productivity, teamwork, job satisfaction, cost, and rate of turnover are measurable variables. A quantitative analysis of these variables showed organizations would benefit from leadership recognition and inclusion of OCB in formal job performance evaluations. The new data obtained in combination with the results of prior literature will assist leaders in discussing the possible need for recognition of OCBs exhibited by employees in the performance evaluation process.

Other variables may exist that can skew the outcome of the research study (Cronk, 2008);

therefore, a full list of variables was necessary in the final analysis. The variables included three groups: independent variables (IV), dependent variables (DV), and control variables (CV), if the three variables existed through the collection and manipulation of data. Variables with little or no effect on the outcome of the study, or outliers, would have been included as part of the statistical data to show the relevant variables were part of the research and testing process. Including some of the outlying variables may have provided validity and reliability to the tests. The minimum suggested statistical methodologies are multiple-regression analysis, ANOVA, a descriptive analysis, and a covariance analysis to determine if any independent or dependent variables affected any identified control variables. Tables and charts were used to assist with reviewing the data analysis methods and outcomes.

The study requirements included capturing data from 115 employees representing each of 10 various healthcare industries in Washington State. Determining the sample population size was calculated using a formula recommended by Tabachnick and Fidell (2001, p. 117):

Sample Size = 104 + n, where n equals the number of independent variables.

Therefore, the sample size for this study required 115 completed survey documents. Various general forms of statistical analysis followed the data collection process that included Pearson t-tests or ANOVA testing. A review of the data determined if any independent or dependent variables existed. The statistical data analysis determined the effect the implementation of a formal process of recognizing and rewarding employees for exhibiting OCB as part of the employee evaluation process on productivity, teamwork, job performance, and satisfaction.

Elaboration of Rationale for Research Method.

The value of performing a quantitative analysis over a qualitative analysis provided an opportunity to collect data and show the results using tables to provide a visual description of the study outcome. Accompanied by a statistical description of the data collection and dissemination of the information in tables, a quantitative study was appropriate to answer the research question.

Research Question.

Q[1]: What effect does leadership recognition of
OCBs in performance evaluations have on
employees' productivity, teamwork, job
performance, and satisfaction?

Hypothesis.

H[1]: There is an increase in productivity, teamwork,
job performance, and satisfaction because of
implementing a formal process of recognizing and
rewarding employees for exhibiting OCB as part of
the employee evaluation process.

Null Hypothesis.

H[o]: There is no increase in productivity, teamwork,
job performance, and satisfaction because of
implementing a formal process of recognizing and
rewarding employees for exhibiting OCB as part of
the employee evaluation process.

Elaboration of Proposed Research Design Appropriateness.

A quantitative study showed that organizations might benefit from leadership recognition and inclusion of organizational citizenship behaviors in formal job performance evaluations. Much of the literature available regarding OCB used a descriptive and quantitative research design. The selected design is descriptive and quantitative because the majority of literature relates to obtaining information about employee productivity, teamwork, job performance, and job satisfaction.

Elaboration of Why the Proposed Design Will Accomplish the Study Goals.

The selected quantitative research design was appropriate because the data from participants: employee productivity, teamwork, job satisfaction, job performance, and rewards can be given a numerical (nominal) value for comparison with other studies. When a numerical value, such as the Likert-type scale (numbers) are given for each variable, the information from participants regarding individual perceptions of productivity, teamwork, job satisfaction, job performance, and recognition became measurable.

Population

The purpose of this descriptive, quantitative study was to analyze the benefit of formally recognizing employees who exhibit OCB as part of the formal performance evaluation process. A random sample of 115 employees representing each of 10 various healthcare industries in Washington State were asked to complete an anonymous and confidential survey. The survey return rate of 82% or higher enabled the survey results to be analyzed. The survey results determined leadership recognition of OCB positively affects employee productivity, teamwork, job performance, job satisfaction, and rewards.

No other research studies revealed if any organizations directly or explicitly recognize OCB as part of the formal reward and recognition system. Several ideas for designing and implementing a performance evaluation process that officially recognizes the value of OCB from more recent literature is available, particularly from the study by Johnson et al. (2009). An employee perception that leaders expect employees to exhibit OCB exists (Chen et al., 2009; Chen & Chiu, 2009). Johnson et al. (2009) acknowledged employees who exhibited OCBs have a *good faith* expectation of a reward for increased contributions, even though the employer is not contractually obligated to provide any pay or benefits over the agreed to pay-for-performance rate during hire. This perception and expectation may come from the added term to official employee job description or task documentation as *other duties as assigned.*

According to Reynolds (2008), the information from the survey may provide employees in all industries to realize if they receive recognition for exhibiting OCBs by leadership. Once employees recognized the additional contributions OCB provided an organization, employees might include additional personal perceptions through participation in the research study. The subject of organizational citizenship behavior requires more research regarding the cost benefit and improvement of implementing

operational systems for formally recognizing and
rewarding employees in organizations that exhibit
OCB.

Sampling and Data Collection

The method of obtaining data was to identify
healthcare organizations in Washington State
regardless of if the organization formally recognized
OCB as part of employee performance evaluations.
Many healthcare organizations declined to participate;
therefore, the survey took place in a parking lot, with
permission from a local grocery store and online. For
those who qualified and agreed to participate in the

study an anonymous survey requesting a personal assessment of individual participant demographics, KSAs, experience, education, OCB, and rating current job satisfaction was provided as a paper or online survey.

Participating individual participants received a definition of OCB in the informed consent document. Requests for participation were sent to several healthcare organizations, but none agreed to participate. Therefore, the modified research instrument requested participants to identify only the healthcare industry in which the participant worked. Participant selection process included verification by participants of employment in healthcare in Washington State and understanding of the process of informed consent.

Informed Consent and Confidentiality

As part of the sampling process, participants in Washington State received information regarding the study. Participants had to acknowledge and understand any foreseeable direct or indirect risks to their health and privacy before providing consent to participate in the study. Although the focus of the research study related to individual behaviors, the use of the research design discovered no incidental findings. An incidental finding concerned an individual research participant with potential health issues discovered while conducting research, but is beyond the aims of the study (Wolf, Paradise, & Caga-anan, 2008, p. 363).

According to Cone and Foster (2006), informed consent and confidentiality are key elements in the ethical execution of a research study. The informed consent document (Appendix C) included: a) a clear statement of the study and the expectations of what information participants will provide, b) how much time the participant needed to complete the survey, c) potential risks and benefits, d) that participation was voluntary and that participants can remove themselves from the study at any time without penalty or loss of benefit by completing the participant withdrawal form and returning it according to the detailed instructions (Appendix D), e) a contact name and phone number if a participant desired to withdraw from the research study, f) a contact name and phone number if a participant desired to file a complaint about the research study, g) if any compensation was available for participating in the research study, h) where and when a summary of the research results will be made available to participants, and i) proper signatures from both the participant and the individual conducting the research (Collaborative Institutional Training Center, 2011). Participants in Washington State also received a statement of assurance of confidentiality as agreed to prior to the commencement of the research and data collection process (Appendix E). Researcher confidentiality is a required form of ethical research conduct (Cone & Foster, 2006).

Instrumentation

Data Collection Instrument.

Fournier (2008, p. 112) provided an
acceptable, validated data collection instrument for a
research study on interactional justice and the effects
of OCB. A copy of the letter requesting permission to
use an existing, validated survey (Appendix F) and
the signed permission to use an existing, validated
survey (Appendix G) allowed the use of the
questionnaire used by Dr. William Fournier in his
doctoral dissertation, *Communication Satisfaction,
Interactional Justice, and Organizational Citizenship
Behaviors: Staff Perceptions in a University
Environment* (2008), construct validity of the research
instrument (Appendix G) is based on the work of
Organ (1988), Van Dyne, Graham, and Dienesch
(1994), Van Dyne, Cummings, & Parks (1995), and
Fournier (2008). The research questions were similar
to the information to perform a descriptive quantitative
study in the subject of OCB. The questionnaire by
Fournier (2008, p. 112) used a Likert-type scale,

which was also useful in the ease of completing this study. Neuman (2003, p. 199) stated the validity, reliability, and strength of a Likert-type scale is because of the simplicity of use by researchers and using behavioral or emotional categories to obtain responses.

A review of other questionnaires from prior studies did not have the same quality and quantity of questions to obtain the most information available on the subject of OCB. Those questionnaires with a Likert-type scale appeared to be the best choice for a quantitative study. Other methods of data gathering, such as Thurstone Scaling, according to Neuman (2003), might not have been useful because of the difficulty associated with analyzing and interpreting the data. Revisions to the data collection instrument were necessary, but were minimal.

Reason for Choosing this Instrument.

A review of other data collection instruments did not provide the quantity or quality of questions in comparison with the Fournier (2008) data collection document (Appendix A). The questions in Fournier's

(2008) research study replicated (with permission to
modify for research purposes) the same data
appropriate for this study on OCBs. Modification of
Fournier's (2008) document was necessary to adapt
to the parameters of the data to complete the
research study regarding OCB. The research
instrument (see Appendix A for notes on reference
source) explained what OCBs are, and requested
ratings by participants of individual performance and
exhibition of the OCB descriptors using a Likert-type
scale. The original research instrument (Appendix A)
was adapted from four prior research studies: Organ
(1977), Smith, Organ, and Near (1983), Van Dyne,
Graham, and Dienesch (1994), and Van Dyne,
Cummings, and Parks (1995), increasing the
construct validity of the research instrument.

Job related information was also requested
based on individual perceptions. The questions
regarding the perception of fairness were appropriate
in relation to job performance, fairness in the
decision-making process of leadership, and the
processes in which employees interacted with leaders
and peers. Collecting data regarding participants'
belief that organizational leaders recognized the

contributions by employees regarding the exhibition of OCBs in performance evaluations is necessary. The perception of fair treatment was an important factor in if employees exhibit OCBs (Mathis & Jackson, 2006; Kreitner, 2004).

Instrument Appropriateness to this Study.

The validated research instrument (Appendix A) was appropriate to this study as the same information gathered by Fournier's (2008) study was relevant and necessary to assist in answering the research question and helped in supporting the hypothesis. The information for this study was similar to the information in Fournier's (2008) study, including the staff perceptions of communication, interactional justice, and OCB. The study reported the responses from participants regarding employee productivity, teamwork, job performance, job satisfaction, and rewards in relation to the lack of recognition of OCB behaviors in job performance evaluations in healthcare organizations in Washington State.

Data Reduction.

All participants were and remain anonymous. Three years from university approval for the study, the data from the study will be destroyed through appropriate and confidential measures. The data for the research study is secured on a USB drive in a locked box in a combination safe. The combination to the safe is known only to the researcher. Under Institutional Review Board (IRB) guidelines, the destruction of the research data for this study will commence three years after study completion through a certified and bonded shredding service.

Validity and Reliability

Internal Validity.

This study used random sampling of intrinsic independent and control variables to not confound the results. An analysis of the measurable dependent variables determined the results were not affected by the independent and control variables. How the data collected denoted the interaction of the variables would have been important to show how each variable affected the study outcome (Black, 2005, p. 57). Most of the possible internal validity factors that could threaten the reliability of the data did not occur. Because the modified survey instrument (Appendix H) allowed participants to provide emotional and behavioral perceptions, participants could not make changes the completed survey document after submission of the modified research instrument. Participants could not retake the survey more than once increasing the randomness of the study responses.

External Validity.

Choosing participants who best represented the population and providing a clear statement of the hypothesis helped with the external validity of the study (Black, 2005, p. 45). The best participants for the research study were employees in the branches of the healthcare industry. The modified survey instrument (Appendix H) contained the elements for analysis, and participants could provide individual feedback. Participants were provided a set of scripted instructions so each participant received the same information (Neuman (2003, p. 256). The possibility existed that some information the participants provided was subjective and were included as part of the research analysis without bias. An effort was made to identify and remove subjective material from the analysis. All information and responses provided by the sample population were included in the data analysis.

Reliability.

The modified survey instrument (Appendix H) was a valid document. The questionnaire was modified for this study from an approved, validated, and published dissertation by Fournier (2008). The validated survey instrument (Appendix A) was modified from previous research completed by Organ (1988), Van Dyne, Graham, and Dienesch (1994), and Van Dyne, Cummings, and Parks (1995). The information obtained in the valid data collection instrument by Fournier (2008) was similar and is consistent to information to complete the research study. The face validity of the data collection instrument was appropriate for this study. No construct validity issues were identified with the valid or modified research documents during or after the research study.

Data Analysis Method

Data analysis software was available to assist with the compilation and sorting of the data from the research study. SPSS software was used to generate statistical reports and tables. Because of the need to report accurate statistical findings, a consultation with a member of the American Statistical Association assisted in reviewing the data analysis results for the study. Ge and Whitmore (2010) suggested using an independent and certified statistician to consult and review the data, lessening researcher bias and calculation errors. During the research process there was an expectation some participants would provide data that could be outlying information. Outlying information can skew the results of these statistical analysis methods: multiple-regression analysis, ANOVA, descriptive analysis, and a covariance analysis (Brown, 2011). No outlying information was identified during the descriptive, quantitative analysis.

Data Analysis Technique Selection Appropriateness to Research Design.

Because a quantitative research design method requires the intricate use and knowledge of statistical analysis, a consultation with a member of the American Statistical Association assisted with determining the appropriate method for the standard deviation and which data analysis process was most appropriate for the study. As part of the analysis process, the certified statistician assisted in checking the validation of the statistical reduction techniques for the analysis in chapter four regarding the findings of what, when, where, why, and how the variables supported the hypothesis and rejected the null hypothesis (Scott & Howell, 2008). The quantitative research design measured employee productivity, teamwork, job performance, job satisfaction, teamwork, and the perception of rewards and recognition. An analysis of the data matching the independent, dependent, and control variables measured the probable impact of leadership recognition of OCB.

Summary

The descriptive, quantitative study resulted from literature that suggested employees and employers are aware OCB exists, which created an expectation that exhibition of OCBs by employees are an integral part of general employee contributions

(Chen et al., 2009; Chen & Chiu, 2009; Johnson et al.). A random sample of 115 employees representing each of 10 various healthcare industries in Washington State provided a better understanding of the expectations of OCBs. The findings revealed how OCB affected employee productivity, teamwork, job performance, job satisfaction, and rewards in relation to the lack of recognition of OCB behaviors in job performance evaluations. The discoveries from the random survey formed the basis of analysis and discussion for chapter four.

CHAPTER IV

FINDINGS

This chapter presents the results of the data collected using a descriptive, quantitative research method to analyze the benefit of formally recognizing employees who exhibited organizational citizenship behaviors as part of the formal performance evaluation process. The data represents a purposive sample of 115 employees representing each of 10 various healthcare industries, to include employees holding management and non-management positions in healthcare organizations in Washington State. The findings from the data analysis answered whether or not leadership recognition of OCB was positively related to employee productivity, teamwork, job satisfaction, and rewards. The data analysis was organized according to a case review of the research question and hypothesis, rate of response and demographics, findings, validity, and reliability of the

research instrument, and descriptive analysis of the
sample, and the report of data gathered for the
research question.

Response Rate and Demographics.

Fournier (2008) conducted a study titled
*Communication Satisfaction, Interactional Justice,
and Organizational Citizenship Behaviors: Staff
Perceptions in a University Environment* to "measure
the perception of extra-role behavior (organizational
citizenship behaviors) and perception of fairness in
relationships (interactional justice), and
communications satisfaction" among leaders in a
university setting (abstract). The validated research

instrument provided by Fournier (2008) (Appendix A) was modified to fit the needs of this study by a) removing all references to the *university* in questions 20, 29, 30, 31, and 34, b) entirely removing questions 11, 19, 25, 26, 39, 44, 41, c) revising demographic question 70 to list the 10 healthcare industry constructs, and d) revising the Likert-type scale from seven responses to five responses. Because the modifications to the validated research instrument were minimal, Black (2005, p. 273) suggested that the modified instrument is likely to be stable and produce similar results, as if the survey were conducted under similar circumstances. After the deletions and changes, the modified survey instrument (Appendix H) contained 60 questions and was created online through Zoomerang™, an online survey generation tool that provides secure links to online surveys. The survey was provided to participants as a paper and electronic survey.

Appendix I contains the survey constructs, a breakdown of the number of survey questions that pertained to one of the six variables in the research question: leadership recognition of OCB (20), OCBs (4), productivity (11), teamwork (5), job performance

(8), and job satisfaction (1). The remaining seven questions provided demographic information about the participants. The modified survey instrument (Appendix H) was provided as a four-page printed document and online to available participants who met the qualifications: a) 18 years or older, b) worked in the healthcare industry in Washington State, c) agreed to participate in the study. All qualifying participants were provided informed consent forms (Appendix C) regarding the benefits and risks of participating in the survey; including the contact information and procedure for withdrawal from the study, and a withdrawal form (Appendix D). The majority of participants elected to participate through the secure website where an informed consent form had to be read and accepted prior to completing the survey.

A total of 118 suitable participants representing employees from 10 various healthcare industries participated in the survey. The data from three partially completed surveys returned during the data collection process are not included in the final analysis. Table 1 displays the frequency counts for the selected variables. Out of 102 participants who

provided gender information, more women (n = 64)
than men (n = 38) responded. The participants ranged
in ages from 18 to over 60 with the most participants
in the 30-39 age group (21%) and 40-49 age group
(29%). The majority of participants received some
college education (64%) and 17% had at least
obtained a bachelor's degree. The most common
reported salary range was $40,000-$49,000 annually
(24%), and the most frequent length of time the
participants have been working in their current
position is about 1-5 years (24%). The majority of
participants worked full-time (64%), held non-
management (42%) or administrative (9%) positions,
and worked in major hospitals (26%). Sixty-seven
percent of participants reported the level of job
satisfaction stayed the same. The level of productivity
stayed the same for 67% of participants. As for the
perception of receiving rewards and recognition from
leadership, 59% of the participants reported they had
not received a raise in pay, a job title promotion or
both a raise in pay and job title promotion.

Table 1 - Frequency Counts for Selected Variables (N = 115)

Variable	Frequency	n	%
Gender			
	Male	38	33
	Female	64	55.7
	Decline to answer	13	11.3
Age			
	18-29	22	19.1
	30-39	24	20.9
	40-49	33	28.7
	50-50	13	11.3
	60 or older	1	0.9
	Decline to answer	22	19.1
Level of Education			
	Did not finish high school	2	1.7
	High school	19	16.5
	Some college, no degree	29	25.2
	Two-year college degree	24	20.9
	Four-year college degree	13	11.3
	Graduate degree	6	5.2
	Post-graduate degree	1	0.9
	Decline to answer	21	18.3
Salary Range			
	Less than $20,000	8	7
	$21-$29,000	13	11.3
	$30-$39,000	25	21.7
	$40-$49,000	27	23.5
	$50-$59,000	11	9.6
	$60-$60,000	1	0.9
	$70-$70,000	2	1.7
	$80,000 or more	1	0.9
	Decline to answer	27	23.5

Table 1- Frequency Counts for Selected Variables
(N = 115) (continued)

Variable	Frequency	n	%
Length of Time in Current Position			
	Less than 1 year	14	12.2
	1-5 years	27	23.5
	6-10 years	25	21.7
	11-15 years	19	16.5
	16-20 years	9	7.8
	26 years or more	1	0.9
	Decline to answer	20	17.4

Table 1: Frequency Counts for Selected Variables (N = 115)

		n	%
Current Position			
	Non-management	48	41.7
	Management	16	13.9
	Administrative	10	8.7
	Licensed medical personnel	19	16.5
	Decline to answer	22	19.1
Job Status			
	Full-time	74	64.3
	Part-time	29	25.2
	On-call	2	1.7
	Temporary	1	0.9
	Decline to answer	9	7.8
Level of Productivity (over past 90 days)			
	Decreased	14	12.2
	Stayed the same	63	54.8
	Increased	38	33
Type of Medical Industry of Employment			
	Major hospital	30	26.1
	Mental health facility	7	6.1
	Assisted living/nursing facility	16	13.9
	Medical office – Adults	8	7
	Dental office	7	6.1
	Chiropractic office	4	3.5

Table 1 - Frequency Counts for Selected Variables
(N = 115) (continued)

Variable	Frequency	n	%
Type of Medical Industry of Employment (cont.)			
	Medical laboratory	3	2.6
	Physical therapy/rehab facility	5	4.3
	Medical office – Pediatrics	4	3.5
	Urgent care facility	4	3.5
	Other - not listed	27	23.5
Level of Job Satisfaction *(over past 90 days)*			
	Decreased	11	9.5
	Stayed the same	77	67
	Increased	27	23.5
Performance Rewards and Recognition Received *(over past 90 days)*			
	Raise in pay	19	16.5
	Job title promotion	8	7
	Raise in pay and job title promotion	20	17.4
	None	68	59.1

Table 2 displays the psychometric characteristics for the six summated scale scores. The Cronbach alpha reliability coefficients ranged from $r = .87$ to $r = .96$ with a median alpha of $r = .92$. These data suggest all scales have adequate levels of internal reliability (Cohen, 1988).

Table 2 - Psychometric Characteristics for Summated Scale Scores (N = 115)

Score	n	M	SD	Low	High	a
Leadership Recognition	20	3.30	0.78	1.65	4.45	0.96
OCB	4	3.63	0.86	1.50	5.00	0.87
Productivity	11	3.34	0.80	1.64	4.82	0.94
Teamwork	5	3.58	0.85	1.40	5.00	0.88
Job Performance	8	3.37	0.79	1.63	5.00	0.92
Satisfaction	1	3.89	0.85	2.00	5.00	n/a[a]

[a] The satisfaction score had one item only, so no Cronbach alpha coefficient was calculated.

Findings

Research Hypothesis.

The research hypothesis predicted there is an increase in productivity, teamwork, job performance, and satisfaction because of implementing a formal process of recognizing and rewarding employees for exhibiting OCB as part of the employee evaluation process, and the null hypothesis, which is there is no increase in productivity, teamwork, job performance, and satisfaction because of implementing a formal process of recognizing and rewarding employees for exhibiting OCB as part of the employee evaluation process. To test this, Table 3 provides the Pearson product-moment correlations among the test variables of leadership recognition, OCB, productivity, teamwork, job performance, and satisfaction.

Table 3 - Inter-Correlations Among Summated Scale Scores (N = 115)

Score	1	2	3	4	5	6
1. Leadership Recognition	1					
2. OCB	0.67	1				
3. Productivity	0.90	0.70	1			
4. Teamwork	0.68	0.77	0.75	1		
5. Performance	0.89	0.67	0.91	0.74	1	
6. Satisfaction	0.56	0.71	0.63	0.70	0.58	1

Note: All correlations are significant at the p < .001 level.

Inspection of the table found all six variables to have significant positive correlations with the other variables at the p <.001 level. The findings provided support for the acceptance of the research hypothesis and rejection of the null hypothesis.

Summary

The survey results indicated there is a significant relationship between leadership recognition of OCBs and employee productivity, performance, teamwork, and satisfaction. A significant percentage of respondents held college degrees, non-management positions, and reported a lack of rewards and recognition in the form of a promotion, pay raise, or both. The analysis of data collected supported the hypothesis: There is an increase in productivity, teamwork, job performance, and satisfaction when implementing a formal process of recognizing and rewarding employees for exhibiting OCB as part of the employee evaluation process.

CHAPTER V
SUMMARY, CONCLUSIONS, AND
RECOMMENDATIONS

The results of the survey indicated employees believe that individual behaviors and actions are of significant value to the organization, but leaders do not provide the needed recognition and rewards to increase employee motivation. This lack of leadership recognition negatively affects the level of satisfaction, productivity, active teamwork, and performance within organizations. The research findings indicated people employed in management positions in the healthcare industry perceived a lack of recognition for their efforts. Therefore, the assumption can be made that regardless of the hierarchical level of employment, recognition, and rewards may be beneficial for increasing the level of satisfaction, productivity, active teamwork, and performance within organizations.

Review of the Research Problem

The answer to the research question asking
what effect leadership recognition of organizational
citizenship behaviors in performance evaluations will
have on employees' productivity, teamwork, job
performance, and satisfaction is that recognition of
OCBs by leaders is recognition does positively affect
the productivity of employees who exhibit OCBs.
Responses to the survey indicate employees know
organizational leaders lack a formal process to
recognize and reward the value-added by employees
who exhibit OCB. The descriptive, quantitative study
supported the hypothesis that formally recognizing
employees who exhibit OCB as part of the formal
performance evaluation process in may be a
significant addition to organizational policies. The
research can be replicated across various industries
on a global scale with the probability of indicating this
phenomenon exists in all areas of business (Black,
2005).

The results of the research study are important
from a leadership perspective because the data
suggests when employees are recognized and

rewarded for contributions toward organizational goals – performance increases. In the research conducted by Fournier (2008) the results regarding OCB indicate employee awareness and perception of exhibiting OCB is positive. No modifications of the theory of OCBs were necessary as supporting research of OCBs by Smith et al (1983), Chen et al. (2009), and others, is related to the social exchange theory by Emerson (1976). One possible alternative explanation for the results is other variables may have been overlooked, omitted, or unidentified during the literature research process.

Summary of the Literature.

Several bodies of literature uphold the research study findings a correlation exists between leadership recognition of OCBs and an increase in productivity, job performance, teamwork, and job satisfaction. Research conducted by Sun et al. (2007) supported the hypothesis that high-performance practices are positively related to service-oriented OCB and that OCB positively influences the relationships between human resources practices, productivity, and turnover. Further research by Chen and Chiu (2009) upheld the argument that organizational leaders lack the formal process to recognize and reward the value-added by employees who exhibit OCBs. Implementation of programs to include leadership recognition and rewards of OCBs outside the normally required job performance descriptions is the next logical step. Implementing reward and recognition programs may increase employees' desire to be productive, work as part of a team, improve general job task performance, and increase professional and personal job satisfaction as stated by Allen (2009).

To further support the need and expectation of implementing formal recognition and rewards programs a study led by Johnson et al. (2009) explored employee perceptions of adding OCB as a weighted part of job performance evaluations. The study indicated employees agree OCB should be recognized by company leadership as part of the formal performance evaluation process. The statistical results of research by Johnson et al. (2009) also indicated employees believe circa 25% of employees' job performance evaluations should recognize that employee's performance over *and above* the tasks they are expected to perform. Employees also stated an expectation that organizations already include OCB as a standard part of the performance evaluation process (Johnson, et al., 2009, p. 409).

Contributions made by employees through behaviors inherent to the values and norms of individuals deserve to be recognized, according to research conducted by Chi and Tsai (2006). Organizational productivity is directly correlated to the recognition and rewards provided to employees who exhibit behaviors not normally included in formal job descriptions. The research shows when employees are recognized and rewarded, employees exhibited a high level of job satisfaction and productivity. Chiu and Tsai (2006) and Jha and Jha (2009) discussed the negative implications of not recognizing employee contributions, including the decrease in productivity of organizations because of a lack of morale among employees.

A strong need exists for organizational leaders to recognize employee contributions through organizational training, design, and cultures. Davis (1996) and Collins (1997) suggested leaders should thoroughly examine rules, roles, norms, and values that may assist in building a strong and stable organization. Kuvaas (2007; 2008) and Dysvik and Kuvaas (2008) studied the employee and leadership behaviors within organizations. The results provided evidence that superior organizational performance is achieved "when employees exert energy on behalf of the organization ... fulfilling employee needs and generating favorable attitudes and behaviors that result in increased performance" (p. 2). When leaders recognize a *job well done*, the recognition of these behaviors (OCBs) determines and defines the extent to which employees believe they are members of an organization (Scott & Davis, 2007, p. 151).

The transformation of organizations into high-performance workplaces requires the recognition of specific individual contributions, including OCBs (Hesselbein et al., 1997, p. 5). As part of the new organizational shift in recognizing employee contributions, Schmidt (2007, p. 282) stated employees who believe they are important members of organizations, through training and development they receive as part of their job performance, are more satisfied and more productive for the organization. Li, Liang, and Crant (2010) substantiated the results of research conducted by Schmidt (2007) by proving the hypothesis that employees relate OCBs to individual job success and satisfaction. Buntzman and Parker's (2008) conclusion of the employee perspective is lack of recognition and rewards can affect the job satisfaction, performance, and retention in organizations.

Research that disagreed with the findings included results reported by Culbert (2010) who deconstructed the performance review process and stated the leadership and employee perception of recognition and rewards is negative. Many employees reported a sense of dread at the thought of receiving negative job performance feedback during the formal performance review process. Leaders reported a perception of negativity from employees from hearing negative comments by employees relating to the impending performance review. Culbert (2010) strongly suggested organizations stop using the performance review as a job evaluation process that is detrimental to motivation and negatively influences employee performance and satisfaction.

Supporting the assumptions made by Culbert (2010), Buntzman and Parker (2008) discussed the leadership perspective of providing recognition and rewards for employee performance reviews. From a leadership perspective the research concluded that recognition and rewards do not influence employee perceptions of employee value to the organization (Buntzman & Parker, 2008). Some employees' perceptions indicate recognition and rewards do not improve the clarity of expectations in performing to the benefit of attaining the organizational mission and values. With this extremely opposite perspective of recognition and rewards, positive views, and actions by leadership equals positive employee perceptions; the converse for negativity (Buntzman & Parker, 2008, p. 82).

Some research discovered recognition and rewards for employee contributions are not always necessary or conducive to organizational success. Podsakoff et al. (2009) discussed the inclusion of counterproductive work habits as part of employee performance reviews. Unhealthy or non-productive employee activities discussed in performance reviews and might decrease employee performance and satisfaction. Colbert (2010, p. 207) agreed with Podsakoff et al. (2009) that recognition and rewards undermines the leader-follower relationship in organizations because some employees may perceive the performance review as punishment. Colbert (2010) stated, "Performance reviews create a competition between boss and subordinate […] take away the performance review, and the relationship changes from competitive to collaborative" (p. 156). The conclusions of Podsakoff, Whiting, Podsakoff, and Blume (2009) and Colbert (2010) were refuted by Spector, Bauer, and Fox (2010) concluding: "counterproductive behaviors and OCBs are unrelated" (p. 781). However, there appears to be agreement in some of the literature that social behaviors may have a negative or a positive effect on organizational processes and performance.

A gap exists between the positive and negative aspects of leadership recognition of OCBs. Previous research and literature exist to argue for and against the need for leadership recognition of OCBs; therefore, this research study can be a guide for organizational leaders. The argument for leadership recognition of OCBs clearly states employees' productivity and job satisfaction increase as they are recognized for a job well done. However, the arguments against leadership recognition of OCBs state some organizations may endure a negative benefit in recognizing employees who exhibit OCBs. The decision to include the recognition of OCBs in performance evaluations should be included in the job performance qualifications assigned to specific positions as the organization recruits and hires new employees. This step may lessen the gap in recognizing OCBs, and create a map and timeline of which industries fall into the positive or negative portion of the gap. Without further research specific to the positive and negative effects of rewards, recognition, and performance reviews, the difference between the positive and negative social behaviors toward the goals of organizations and personal growth of employees could remain unclear.

Scope

A printed survey questionnaire packet and a secure online survey site were used to obtain data for the study. After offering the printed survey to prospective participants, the majority of respondents indicated a desire to participate in the research study electronically. Some participants stated the web-based survey would be more convenient and private.

Because the questionnaire was created using a secure web-based survey production organization (Zoomerang™), qualifying participants were provided the link to the electronic modified survey instrument (Appendix H), a copy of the informed consent (Appendix C), and participant withdrawal form (Appendix D). It was anticipated the research project would take approximately six weeks. The in-person recruiting of random, qualified participants for the data collection process began on March 24, 2012, the web-based site became available to participants on March 26, 2012, and the data collection process concluded on April 26, 2012.

The first page of the web-based survey site requires the participant to reread the informed consent form (Appendix C), attesting to qualifications for participation including: a) working in the healthcare industry in Washington State, b) be over the age of 18, c) understand the risks and benefits of participation, d) understand the process for withdrawal from the study without consequences, and e) understand the survey data provided will be kept confidential, stored securely for three years, and will be destroyed through a secure data destruction organization, and f) the data collected will be used for publication. The selection of the button to continue to the survey questionnaire is the reaffirmation of these qualifications. The survey site questionnaire was visited 148 times, of that 118 surveys were started, three were not completed, and 115 qualified to include in the data analysis.

Limitations

Problems that occurred during the data collection process were minimal. The original sample population of 250 surveys were initially identified as the target sample size and was more than twice that was necessary to complete the data analysis. Further research concluded that collecting and using a smaller sample population of 115 surveys, based on a formula by Tabachnick and Fidell (2011, p. 117) would provide an opportunity for accurate results. The possibility of respondents' requesting to withdraw from the study was anticipated, but was minimal up to the conclusion of the data analysis. Less than five surveys were returned incomplete. Other limitations of choosing the wrong data analysis or reporting method were unfounded.

Other methodologies or factors could cause different conclusions, such as the industry itself. The research study based on the healthcare industry may have the same results as conducting a study for the population of people employed in assembly work. A quantitative study limited participants' responses only to personal and intrinsic beliefs and perceptions.

The analysis may have shown a significant positive relation among the study variables if a participant had a personal bias toward a supervisor or personal contributions to the organization. With this understanding, a different research study using a qualitative method may have generated different results through direct interviews and observation of employees where further responses or activities pertaining to the survey questions would indicate leaders recognizing and rewarding employees for daily accomplishments that employees may notice or perceive as rewards and recognition.

Delimitations.

The information obtained in the data collection results did not provide specific values on OCB, or study a specific person or organization. Discoveries from the study are only a tool for organizations to implement process improvements, but in no way suggests the ideas or theories in the study are the best information available for organizations. The study is not designed nor does it create new theories on OCB. The study results may provide ideas that may assist leaders with expanding on ways to use OCB to the best benefit of organizations and human resources needs. Some ideas can be helpful tools for leadership to recognize and reward employees who exhibit OCBs through implementing changes to organizational employee performance evaluations.

Modified Survey Instrument.

The validated survey instrument (Appendix A) used in the research study was adapted and modified from one used by Fournier (2008) with permission. After review of many research instruments from previous studies, the one by Fournier (2008) most closely matched the needs of the survey in addressing organizational citizenship behaviors. The questions from Fournier's (2008) previously validated survey instrument (Appendix A) met the needs of the research study, with a few exceptions. Some of the original questions were deleted because they did not pertain to the healthcare industry and other questions were modified to remove the word *university*, yet the questions related to OCBs. The re-wording of some questions was necessary to meet the requirements of the survey topic.

Lack of Pilot Study.

Several factors can be attributed to the lack of conducting a pilot study to obtain data for the research study. Due to the availability of several previous research studies on the subject of organizational citizenship behaviors, it was determined a pilot study was unnecessary. The previous research instrument used by Organ (1988) and modified by Van Dyne, Graham, and Dienesch (1994), Van Dyne, Cummings, and Parks (1995), and Fournier (2008), in the continued research of OCB provided construct validity to the document. Using the information from a pilot study may have been beneficial in supporting the hypothesis; however, the lack of validation for the pilot study questions may have been a false indicator of proving or disproving the hypothesis. Using the previously tested and valid survey instrument (Appendix A) (Fournier, 2008) that also addressed the subject of OCBs lessened the probability of bias (Black, 2005).

Conclusions and Implications

Organizational leaders must step back and realize that the saying, *happy employees are productive employees,* is a truthful statement. If employees perceive no sense of value and recognition for the work they accomplish, the result for the organization may be lack of productivity. A simple pat on the back can be an extremely cost-effective way to encourage and increase employee productivity. By recognizing and rewarding even the smallest accomplishment by employees toward organizational goals, organizational leaders are building a foundation of trust and camaraderie that will only strengthen the entire organization.

Another reason to include OCBs in performance evaluations is to recognize the intrinsic personal value of good citizenship in the workplace. Encouraging employees when they perform tasks on an altruistic level; doing things for others without prompting may become a useful tool for increasing productivity and performance, and enabling team-building across the organization. Building a circle of reciprocal trust between employees and organizational leaders may be a difficult and daunting task given the global economic situation.

Shareholders, boards of directors, employees, organizational leaders, and entire communities are affected by the success or failure of an organization. Shareholders expect a return on the monetary and physical investments made toward the organization's growth. Boards of directors and organizational leaders are charged with recognizing and implementing processes that meet or exceed the expectations of the shareholders. Communities expect organizations to help with the economic flow of goods and services by employing residents who purchase goods and services from other organizations within the community. These expectations rest on the happiness and productivity of employees. Leadership recognition of employees' citizenship behaviors may be a cost-effective way to meet the most important and specific expectation of shareholders and communities: increase revenue.

Recommendations for Future Research

Replication of the study with different samples or populations is possible using the same survey questions and only changing the demographic inquiry of job or industry type. Removing the response of licensed medical personnel from question 58, and changing the response parameters from the 10 listed healthcare industries to retail or service industries for question 60, it may be possible to obtain the same results. Checking for alternative or new variables may be helpful in further proving results and to strengthen the fixed variables found throughout a literature review.

With more time and resources the scope and limitations could be lessened. For short-term organizational goals, implementing in-service training or pilot programs and tracking the results of the programs may show either a positive or negative change in organizational productivity. The results of the training or pilot program can helped to design a reward and recognition program tailored for the specific organization or industry. Conversely, the training and pilot program could reveal a negative benefit to the organization. Results from the training and pilot programs will only take a short amount of time to reveal the need or lack of need to change organizational policies and procedures. The training and pilot programs also may be a cost-saving project to identify whether a need for leadership recognition processes exists. The study only covers aspects of OCB theory. Further research is warranted to take the subject to a new level.

REFERENCES

Allen, J. F. (2009). Building a Group into a Team. *The Internet Journal of Healthcare Administration, 6*(3). http://dx.doi.org/10.5580/2568 Retrieved from

Andolsen, A. A. (2008). The ingredients of a good leader. *Information Management Journal, 42*(6), 31-46. Retrieved from

Azuka, E. B. (2009). Ethics of leadership and the integrity question among leaders. *Ife Psychologia, 17*(1), 11-26. http://dx.doi.org/10.4314/ifep.v17i1.43736

Baeza, A. H., Lao, C. A., Meneses, J. G., & Roma, V. G. (2009). Leader charisma and affective team climate: The moderating role of the leader's influence & interaction. *Psicothema, 21*(4), 515-520. http://dx.doi.org/10.1037/e518422013-671

Black, T. R. (2005). *Doing quantitative research in the social sciences: An integrated approach to research design, measurement and statistics.* Thousand Oaks, CA: Sage Publications.

Boichuk, J. P. (2010). *When job dissatisfaction leads to customer-oriented citizenship behaviors* (Masters Thesis). Brock University. ISBN 978-0-494-58240-4

Borial, O., Caer, M., & Baron, C. (2009). The action logics of environmental leadership: A developmental perspective. *Journal of Business Ethics, 85*(4), 479-499. doi:10.1007/s10551-008-9784-2

Bonini, S., Koller, T., & Mirvis, P. (2009). Valuing social responsibility programs. *McKinsey Quarterly,* (4), 65-73.

Bowen, D. E., & Inkpen, A. C. (2009). Exploring the role of "global mindset" in leading change in international contexts. *Journal of Applied Behavioral Science, 45*(2), 239-260. doi:10.1177/0021886309334149

Brink, T. L. (1991). Corporate cultures: A color coding metaphor. *Business Horizons, 34*(5), 39-45. http://dx.doi.org/10.1016/0007-6813(91)90045-w

Brown, D. R. (2011). *An experiential approach to organizational development.* San Francisco: Prentice Hall.

Buntzman, G., & Parker, R. D. (2008). Toward a management strategy for optimal recruiting: Potential applicant concerns on goodness of fit in the corporate culture. *Academy of Strategic Management Journal, 7*, 81-93.

Carson, J. B., Tesluk, P. E., & Marrone, J. A. (2007). Shared leadership in teams: An investigation of antecedent conditions and performance. *Academy of Management Journal 50*(5), 1217-1234. doi:10.2307/20159921

Chen, C., & Chiu, S. (2009). The mediating role of job involvement in the relationship between job characteristics and organizational citizenship behavior. *The Journal of Social Psychology, 149*(4), 474-494. http://dx.doi.org/10.3200/socp.149.4.474-494

Chen, G., & Klimoski, R. J. (2007). Training and development of human resources at work: Is the state of our science strong? *Human Resource Management Review, 17*(2), 180-190. doi:10.1016/j.hmr2007.03.004

Chen, L., Niu, H., Wang, Y., Yang, C., & Tsaur, S. (Fall, 2009). Does job standardization increase organizational citizenship behavior? *Public Personnel Management, 38*(3) 39-49.

Chiaburu, D. S., Oh, I., Berry, C. M., Li, N., & Gardner, R. G. (2011). The five-factor model of personality traits and organizational citizenship behaviors: A meta-analysis. *Journal of Applied Psychology, 96*(6), 1140-1166. http://dx.doi.org/10.1037/a0024004

Chiocchio, F. (March, 2007). Project team performance: A study of electronic task and coordination communication. *Project Management Journal, 38*(1), 97-109.

Cohen, J. (1988). *Statistical power analysis for behavioral* sciences (2nd ed.). New Jersey: Lawrence Erlbaum.

Cohn, J., Katzenbach, J., & Vlak, G. (2008). Finding and grooming breakthrough innovators. *Harvard Business Review, 86*(12), 68-76.

Colbert, A. E., & Wiit, L. A. (2007). The role of goal-focused leadership in enabling the expression of conscientiousness. *Journal of Applied Psychology, 94*(3), 790-796. doi:10.1037/a0014187

Collaborative Institutional Training Initiative (CITI). (2011). Human *research curriculum: Social and behavioral research training.* Retrieved November 7, 2011, from www.citiprogram.org

Collins, D. (1997). The ethical superiority and inevitability of participatory management as an organizational system. *Organization Science, 8*(5), 488-507.

http://dx.doi.org/10.1287/orsc.8.5.489

Cooke, N. J., Gorman, J. C., Duran, J. L., & Taylor, A. R. (2007). Team cognition in experience command-and-control teams. *Journal of Experimental Psychology/Applied, 13*(3), 146-157. doi:10.1037/1076-898X.13.3.146

Cooper, D. R., & Schindler, P. S. (2002). *Business research methods* (8th ed.). Boston, MA: Irwin.

Cronk, B. C. (2008). *How to use SPSS: A step-by-step guide to analysis and interpretation* (5th ed.). Glendale, CA: Pyrzack Publishing:

Culbert, S. A. (2010). *Get rid of the performance review! How companies can stop intimidating, start managing-and focus on what really matters.* New York, NY: Business Plus.

Cunliffe, A. L. (2008). Orientations to social constructionism: Relationally-responsive social constructionism and its implications for knowledge and learning. *Management Learning, 39,* 123-139. doi:10.1177/1350507607087578

Cunliffe, A. L. (2009). The philosopher leader: On relationism, ethics, and reflexivity - A critical perspective to teaching leadership. *Management Learning, 40,* 87-101. doi:10.1177/1350507608099315

Davis, C. R. (1996). The administrative rational model and public organization theory. *Administration & Society, 28*(1), 39-60. Retrieved from http://dx.doi.org/10.1177/0095399 79602800102

Dreachslin, J., & Hobby, F. (2008). Racial and ethnic disparities: Why diversity leadership matters. *Journal of Healthcare Management, 53*(1), 8-13.

Dysvik, A., & Kuvaas, B. (2008). The relationship between perceived training opportunities, work motivation and employee outcomes. *International Journal of Training and Development, 12*(3), 138-157. http://dx.doi.org/10.1111/j.1468-2419.2008.00301.x

Emerson, R. M. (1976). Social exchange theory. *Annual Review of Sociology, 2*(1), 335-362. http://dx.doi.org/10.1146/annurev.so.02.080176.002003

Feldman, S. P. (1996). The ethics of shifting ties: Management theory and the breakdown of culture in modernity. *Journal of Management Studies, 33*(3), 283-299. http://dx.doi.org/10.1111/j.1467-6486.1996.tb00803.x

Ferris, G. R., Hochwarter, W. A., Buckley, M. R., Harrell-Cook, G., & Frink, D. D. (1999). Human resources management: Some new directions. *Journal of Management, 25*(3), 385-415.

http://dx.doi.org/10.1177/014920639902500306

Fiol, C. M., Pratt, M. G., & O'Conner, E. J. (2009). Managing intractable
identity conflicts. *Academy of Management Review, 34*(1), 32-
55. Doi:10.5465/AMR.2009.35713276

Fournier, W. H. (2008). *Communication satisfaction, interactional
justice, and organizational citizenship behaviors: Staff
perceptions in a university environment* (Doctoral Dissertation).
UMI Number 3319021. Retrieved from
http://search.proquest.com.ezproxy.apollolibrary.com/dissertati
ons/docview/89263797/12DB56BF26F15EC64BE/5?accountid
=35812

Galbraith, J. R. (1974). Organization design: An information processing
view. *Interfaces, European Institute for Advanced Studies,
4*(3), 28-36. http://dx.doi.org/10.1287/inte.4.3.28

Ge, W., & Whitmore, G. A. (2010). Binary response and logistic
regression in recent accounting research publications: A
methodological note. *Revised Quantitative Financial
Accounting, 34*, 81-93. doi:10.1007/s11156-009-0123-1

George, J. M., & Zhou, J. (2007). Dual tuning in a supportive context:
Joint contributions of positive mood, negative mood, and
supervisory behaviors to employee creativity. *Academy of
Management Journal, 50*(3), 605-622.
http://dx.doi.org/10.5465/amj.2007.25525934

Giblin, E. J., & Amuso, L. E. (Winter, 1997). Putting meaning into
corporate values. Business Forum, *22*(1), 14-18.

Grant, A. M. (2008). Does intrinsic motivation fuel the prosocial fire?
Motivational synergy in predicting persistence, performance, &
productivity. *Journal of Applied Psychology, 93*(1), 48-58. doi:
10.1037/0021-9010.93.1.48

Hesselbein, F., Goldsmith, M., & Beckhard, R. (eds.). (1997). The
organization of the future. New York, NY: The Peter F. Drucker
Foundation for Nonprofit Management.

Hickman, G. R. (2010). *Leading organizations: Perspectives for a new
era (*2nd ed.). Thousand Oaks, CA: SAGE Publications.

Holt, S., Bjorklund, R., & Green, V. (2009). Leadership and culture:
Examining the relationship between cultural background and
leadership perceptions. *Journal of Global Business Issues,
3*(2), 149-164.

Ilies, R., Judge, T., & Wagner, D. (2006). Making sense of motivational
leadership: The trail from transformational leaders to motivated
followers. *Journal of Leadership and Organizational Studies,
13*(1), 1-22. http://dx.doi.org/10.1177/10179190701300010301

Jana, J. (2009). The summit 2005, "Change *is inevitable--growth is intentional.* PsycEXTRA A & D Highlights, 3(1), 3. http://dx.doi.org/10.1037/e636552007-005

Jha, S., & Jha, S. (2009). Determinants of organizational citizenship behaviour: A review of literature. *Journal of Management & Public Policy, 1*(1), 33-42.

Johnson, A. (2008). The influence of need for achievement, need for affiliation, leadership support, and organizational culture on organizational citizenship behavior (Doctoral Dissertation). *ProQuest Dissertation & Theses.* Retrieved from: http://search.proquest.com.ezproxy. apollolibrary.com/dissertations/docview/304835462/fulltextPDF /12DBE33DD7A28E2B713/1?accountid=35812

Johnson, S. K., Holladay, E., & Quinones, M. A. (2009). Organizational citizenship behavior in performance evaluations: Distributive justice or injustice? *Journal of Business Psychology, 24,* 409-418. doi:10.1007/s10869-009-9118-0

Jones, G. R. (2004). *Organizational theory, design, and change* (1st ed.). Upper Saddle River, NJ: Prentice-Hall.

Judge, T. A., & Bono, J. E. (2000). Five-factor model of personality and transformational leadership. *Journal of Applied Psychology, 85*(5), 751-765. doi:10.1037//0021-9010.85/5/751

Keeffee, M. J., Darling, J. R., & Natesan, N. C. (2008). Effective 360 management enhancement: The role of style in developing a leadership team. *Organization Development Journal, 26*(2), 89-107.

Kegan, R., & Laley, L. L. (2009). *Immunity to change: How to overcome it & unlock the potential in yourself and your organization.* Boston, MA: Harvard Business Press.

Khilji, S. E., & Wang, X. (2006). "Intended" and "implemented" HRM: The missing linchpin in strategic human resource management research. *International Journal of Human Resource Management, 17(7),* 1171-1189. doi:10.1080 /09585190600756384

Kinicki, A., & Kreitner, R. (2006). Organizational *behavior: Key concepts, skills, and best practices* (2nd ed.). New York, NY: McGraw Hill, Irwin.

Kivlighan, D. M. (1997). Leader behavior and therapeutic gain: An application of situational leadership theory. *Group Dynamics: Theory, Research, and Practice, 1*(1), 32-38. doi:10.1037/1089-2699.1.1.32

Kreitner, R. (2004). Management (9th ed.). Boston, MA: Houghton Mifflin

Company.

Kuvaas, B. (2007). Different relationships between perceptions of developmental performance appraisal and work performance. *Personnel Review, 36*(3), 378-397. doi:10.1108/00483480710731338

Kuvaas, B. (2008). An exploration of how the employee-organization relationship affects the linkage between perception of developmental human resource practices and employee outcomes. *Journal of Management Studies, 45*(1), 1-25. doi:10.1111/j.1467-6486.2007. 00710.x

Laurie, D., & Lynch, R. (2007). Aligning HR to the CEO growth agenda. *Human Resource Planning, 30*(4), 25-33.

Lee, Y., & Chang, H. (2008). Relations between teamwork and innovation in organizations and the job satisfaction of employees: A factor analytic study. *International Journal of Management, 25*(3), 732-739.

Leon, G. R., Kanfer, R., Hoffman, R. G., & Dupre, L. (1994). Group processes and task effectiveness in a Soviet-American expedition team. *Environment and Behavior, 26,* 149-165. doi:10.1177/001391659402600201

Li, C., & Hung, C. (2009). The influence of transformational leadership on workplace relationships and job performance. *Social Behavior & Personality, 37*(8), 1129-1142. doi:10.2224/sbp.2009.37.8.1129.

Li, N., Liang, J., & Crant, J. M. (Mar, 2010). The role of proactive personality in job satisfaction and organizational citizenship behavior: A relational perspective. *Journal of Applied Psychology, 95*(2), 395-404.

Legnick-Hall, C. A., & Legnick-Hall, M. L. (1988). Strategic human resources management: A review of the literature and proposed typology. *Academy of Management, The Academy of Management Review Journal, 13*(3), 454-470. http://dx.doi.org/10.5465/amr.1988.4306978

Maital, S., & Seshadri, D. V. R. (2007). Innovation *management: Strategies, concepts and tools for growth and profit.* Thousand Oaks, CA: Response Books.

Mathis, R. L., & Jackson, J. H. (2006). Human resource management (11th ed.). Mason, OH: Thompson-Southwestern.

Mayer, S. J., & Russell, J. S. (1987). Behavior modeling training in organizations: Concerns and conclusions. *Journal of Management, 13*(1), 21-40. http://dx.doi.org/10.1177/014920638701300103

Michalisin, M. D., Karau, S. J., & Tangpong, C. (2007). Leadership's
activation of team cohesion as a strategic asset: An empirical
simulation. *Journal of Business Strategies, 24*(1), 1-26.

Monroe, K. R., Hankin, J., & Van Vechten, R. B. (2000). The
psychological foundation of identity politics. *Annual Review of
Political Science, 3,* 419-497. Retrieved from:
http://dx.doi.org/10.1146/annurev.polisci.3.1.419

Moseley, J. L., & Dessinger, J. C. (Eds.). (2010). *Handbook of
improving performance in the workplace:* Vol.3. Measurement
and evaluation. San Francisco, CA: Pfeiffer

Neuman, W. L. (2003). *Social research methods: Qualitative and
quantitative approaches,* (5th ed.). Boston: MA: Pearson
Education, Inc.

Nishii, L., & Mayer, D. (2009). Do inclusive leaders help to reduce
turnover in diverse groups? The moderating role of leader-
member exchange in the diversity to turnover relationship.
Journal of Applied Psychology, 94(6), 1412-1426.
doi:10.1037/a0017190

Office of Personnel Management. (2015). Assessments: Frequently
asked questions: What are Knowledge, Skills, and Abilities?
Retrieved from: http://www.opm.gov
/FAQs/QA.aspx?fid=de14aff4-4f77-4e17-afaa-
fa109430fc7b&pid=56f30860-6b28-4899-a8f8-
459aa856a077&result=1

Organ, D. W. (1977). A Reappraisal and reinterpretation of the
satisfaction-causes-performance hypothesis. *Academy of
Management Review, 2*(1), 46-53. doi:10.5465/AMR.
1977.4409162

Organ, D. W. (1988). *Organizational citizenship behavior: The good
soldier syndrome* (pp. 1-33). Lexington, KY: D.C. Heath.

Organ, D. W., Podsakoff, P. M., & MacKenzie S. P. (2006).
*Organizational citizenship behavior: Its nature, antecedents,
and consequences.* London: Sage Publications.

Ozen, S., & Kusku, F. (2009). Corporate environmental citizenship
variation in developing countries: An institutional framework.
Journal of Business Ethics, 89(2), 297. doi:10.1007/s10551-
008-0001-0

Parker, G. (2008). *Team players and teamwork: New strategies for
developing successful collaboration, completely updated and
revised* (2nd ed.). San Francisco, CA: Jossey-Bass.

Pavlica, K., Holman, D., & Thorpe, R. (1998). The manager as a
practical author of learning. *Career Development International,*

   3(7), 300-307. doi10.1108/136204 39810240728

Podsakoff, N. P., Whiting, S. W., Podsakoff, P. M., & Blume, B. D. (Jan,
   2009). Individual- and organizational-level consequences of
   organizational citizenship behaviors: A meta-analysis. *Journal
   of Applied Psychology, 94*(1), 122-141.
   http://dx.doi.org/10.1037/a0013079

Randolph, W. A., & Dess, G. G. (1984) The congruence perspective of
   organization design: A conceptual model and multivariate
   research approach. *The Academy of Management Review,
   9*(1), 114-127. doi10.5465/AMR. 1984.4278106

Reynolds, J. F. (2008). The averaged American: Surveys, citizens and
   the making of a mass public. *Journal of Social History, 41*, 767.
   Retrieved from: http://dx.doi.org/ 10.1353/jsh.2008.0063

Richards, P. (2008). Succession planning: Does it matter in the context
   of corporate leadership? *Australian Journal of Adult Learning,
   48*(3), 445-464.

Rosen, R. H., Berger, L., & Tarcher, J. P. (1991). Human resources
   management: The healthy company: Eight strategies to
   develop people, productivity, and profits. *Compensation
   Benefits Review, 24*(78). doi:10.1177/ 088636879202400423

Rowe, M. (2009). Organizational systems for dealing with conflict and
   learning from conflict: Introduction. *Harvard Negotiation Law
   Review, 14*, 233-237.

Rowold, J. (2008). Multiple effects of human resource development
   interventions. *Journal of European Industrial Training, 32*(1),
   32-44. doi:10.1108/ 03090590810846557

Schein, E. H. (1990). Organizational Culture. *American Psychologist,
   45*(2), 109-119. Retrieved from http://dx.
   doi.org/10.1037//0003-066x.45.2.109

Schein, E. H. (1996). Three cultures of management: The key to
   organizational learning. *Sloan Management Review*, 38(1), 9-
   20.

Schiffbauer, J., Barrett O'Brien, J., Timmons, B. K., & Kiarie, W. N.
   (2008). The role of leadership in HRH development in
   challenging public health settings. *Human resources for
   Health*. doi:10.1186/1478-4491-6-23

Schmidt, S. W. (2007). The relationship between satisfaction with
   workplace training and overall job satisfaction. *Human
   Resource Development Quarterly, 18*(4), 481-498.
   doi:10.1002/hrdq.1216

Schoo, A. (2008). Leaders and their teams: Learning to improve
   performance with emotional intelligence and using choice

theory. *International Journal of Reality Therapy, 27*(2), 40-45.

Scott, K. W., & Howell, D. (2008). Clarifying analysis and interpretation in grounded theory: Using a conditional relationship guide and reflective coding matrix. *International Journal of Qualitative Methods, 7*(2), 1-15.

Scott, W. R., & Davis, G. F. (2007). *Organizations and organizing: Rational, natural, and open systems* perspectives. Upper Saddle River, NJ: Prentice Hall.

Shore, L. M., Tetrick, L. E., Lynch, P., & Barksdale, K. (2006). Social and economic exchange: Construct development and validation. *Journal of Applied Social Psychology, 36*(4), 837-867. http://dx.doi.org/10.1111/j.0021-9029.2006.00046.x

Sitzmann, T., Brown, K. G., Casper, W., Ely, K., & Zimmerman, R. D. (2008). A review and meta-analysis of the nomological network of trainee reactions. *Journal of Applied Psychology, 93*(2), 280-295. doi:10.1037/0021-9010.93.2.280

Smith, C. A., Organ, D. W., & Near, J. P. (1983). Organizational citizenship behavior: Its nature and antecedents. *Journal of Applied Psychology, 68,* 653-663. Retrieved from: http://dx.doi.org/10.1037//0021-9010.68.4.653

Snape, E., & Redman, T. (2010). HRM practices, organizational citizenship behaviour, and performance: A multi-level analysis. *Journal of Management Studies, 47*(7), 1219-1247. doi:10.1111/j.1467-6486.2009.00911.x

Spector, P. E., Bauer, J. A., & Fox, S. (2010). Measurement artifacts in the assessment of counterproductive work behavior and organizational citizenship behavior: Do we know what we think we know? *Journal of Applied Psychology, 95*(4), 781-790. doi:10.1037/a0019477

Spitzeck, H. (2009). Organizational moral learning: What, if anything, do corporations learn from NGO critique? *Journal of Business Ethics, 88*(1), 157-173. doi:10.1007/s10551-009-0112-2

Steinberg, W. J. (2008). *Statistic alive!* Los Angeles, CA: Sage Publications.

Summers, D. J., Boje, D. M., Dennehy, R. F., & Rosile, G. A. (1997). Deconstructing the organizational behavior text. *Journal of Management Education, 21*(3), 343-360. http://dx.doi.org/10.1177/105256299702100306

Sun, L., Aryee, S., & Law, K. S. (2007). High-performance human resource practices, citizenship behavior, and organizational performance: A relational perspective. *Academy of*

Management Journal, 50(3), 558-577.
doi:10.5465/AMJ.2007.25525821

Swanson, R. A. (1999). The foundations of performance improvement
and implications for practice. *Advances in Developing Human
Resources,* 1(1), 1-25.
doi:10.1177/152342239900100102

Tabachnick, B. G., & Fidell, L. S. (2001). *Using multivariate statistics* (4th
ed.). Boston: Allyn and Bacon.

Takeuchi, R., Lepak, D. P., Wang, H., & Takeuchi, K. (2007). An
empirical examination of the mechanisms mediating between
high performance work systems and performance of Japanese
organizations. *Journal of Applied Psychology, 92*(4), 1069-
1083.
doi:10.1037/0021-9010.92.4.1069

Thompson, L. L. (2008). *Making the team* (3rd ed.). Upper Saddle River,
NJ: Pearson Prentice Hall.

Toh, S. M., Morgeson, F. P., & Campion, M. A. (2008). Human
resources configurations: Investigating fit with the
organizational context. *Journal of Applied Psychology, 93*(4),
864-882. doi:10.1037/0021-9010.93.4.864

Van Aken, J. E. (2007). Design science and organization development
interventions: Aligning business and humanistic values.
Journal of Applied Behavioral Science, 43(1), 67.
doi:10.1177/0021886306297761.

Van Dyne, L., Graham, J., & Dienesch, R. (1994). Organizational
citizenship behavior: Construct redefinition, measurement, and
validation. *Academy of Management Journal, 37*, 765-802.
http://dx.doi.org/10.2307/256600

Van Dyne, L., Cummings, L. L., & Parks, J. M. (1995). Extra-role
behaviors: In pursuit of construct and definitional clarity (a
bridge over muddied waters). *Research in Organizational
Behavior, 17*, 215-285.

Vansteenkiste, M., Neyrinck, B., Niemiec, C., Soenens, B., De Witte, H.,
& Van den Broeck, A. (2007). On the relations among work
value orientations, psychological need satisfaction and job
outcomes: A self-determination theory approach. *Journal of
Occupational and Organizational Psychology* 80(2), 251-277.
doi:10.1348/ 096317906X111024.

Von Bertalanffy, L. (1972). The history and status of general systems
theory. Academy *of Management Journal (pre-1986), 15*(4),
407-426. http://dx.doi.org/10.2307/255139

Wang, Y., & Huang, T. (2009). The relationship of transformational leadership with group cohesiveness and emotional intelligence. *Social Behavior and Personality: An International Journal, 37*(3), 379-392. doi:10.1177/1534484308330018

Willer, D., Lovaglia, M. J., & Markovsky, B. (1997). Power and influence: A theoretical bridge. *Social Forces, 76*(2), 571-603. http://dx.doi.org/10.1093/sf/76.2.571

Wolf, S. M., Paradise, J., & Caga-anan, C. (2008). The law of incidental findings in human subject's research: Establishing researchers' duties. *Journal of Law, Medicine & Ethics, 36*(2), 361-383. http://dx.doi.org/ 10.1111/j.1748-720x.2008.00281.x

Yaghoubi, E., Mashinchi, S. A., Hadi, A. (2011). An Analysis of Correlation between organizational citizenship behavior (OCB) and emotional intelligence (EI). *Modern Applied Science*, 5(2), 119-123. doi:10.5539/mas.v5n2p119

Yukl, G. (1999). An evaluation of conceptual weaknesses in transformational and charismatic leadership theories. *Leadership Quarterly, 10*(2), 285-305. http://dx.doi.org/10.1016/s1048-9843(99)00013-2

Yukl, G. (2010). *Leadership in organizations* (7th ed.). Upper Saddle River, NJ: Pearson Prentice Hall.

Zhang, Z., Hempel, P. S., Han, Y., & Tjosvold, D. (2007). Transactive memory system links work team characteristics and performance. *Journal of Applied Psychology, 92*(6), 1722-1730. doi:10.1037/0021-9010.92.6.1722

APPENDICES

APPENDIX A – Validated Research Instrument

The original copyrighted and validated research instrument was used with permission in this study on November 15, 2011, originating from the dissertation titled, "Communication Satisfaction, Interactional Justice, and Organizational Citizenship Behaviors: Staff Perceptions in a University Environment," by William Fournier, Ph.D., 2008. Copyright 2008 by ProQuest.

Because permissions to use the survey were only provided once for use in researching in this dissertation study, copyright restrictions prevent the instrument from being reproduced here in full. Please see the Dr. Fournier's dissertation for details.

APPENDIX B – Human Subjects (CITI)
Certification

COLLABORATIVE INSTITUTIONAL
TRAINING INITIATIVE (CITI)

Human Resource Curriculum Completion Report
Printed 11/7/2011

Learner: Julie Griffin
Institution: University of Phoenix
Contact: (redacted for privacy)
Information: (redacted for privacy)

Group 1. Social / Behavioral Research Investigator and Key Personnel:
Complete all required modules. Complete optional modules if they pertain to your research activities.

Stage 2. Refresher Course Passed on 11/07/11

Required Modules	Date Complete	Score
Biomedical 101 Refresher Course – Introduction	11/06/11	no quiz
SBR 101 REFRESHER MODULE 1 – History and Ethics	11/07/11	5/5 (100%)
SBR 101 REFRESHER MODULE 2 – Regulatory Overview	11/07/11	5/5 (100%)
SBR 101 REFRESHER MODULE 3 – Risk, Informed Consent, and Privacy and Confidentiality	11/07/11	5/5 (100%)

Required Modules	Date Complete	Score
SBR 101 REFRESHER MODULE 4 – Vulnerable Subjects	11/07/11	4/4 (100%)
SBR 101 REFRESHER MODULE 5 – Education, International, and Internet Research	11/07/11	5/5 (100%)
How to Complete The CITI Refresher Course and Receive the Completion Report	11/07/11	no quiz

For this Completion Report to be valid, the learner listed about must be affiliated with a CITI participating institution. Falsified information and unauthorized use of the CITI course site is unethical, and may be considered misconduct by your institution.

Paul Braunschweiger Ph.D.
Professor, University of Miami
Director Office of Research Education
CITI Course Coordinator

Note: The information above is a facsimile of the original printed pdf document and reproduced here in as close a format as the original for clarity and easier readability.

APPENDIX C – Informed Consent Form

UNIVERSITY OF PHOENIX

INFORMED CONSENT: PARTICIPANTS 18 YEARS OF AGE AND OLDER

Dear Participant,

My name is Julie D. Griffin and I am a student at the University of Phoenix working on a doctoral degree. I am conducting a research study entitled *Leadership Recognition of Organizational Citizenship Behaviors in Performance Evaluations in Washington State Healthcare Organizations*. The purpose of the research study is to study leadership recognition of organizational citizenship behaviors in the formal performance evaluation process. I want to determine if employee productivity, teamwork, job satisfaction, and rewards are related to leadership formally recognizing employees who exhibit organizational citizenship behaviors as part of the performance evaluation process. The significance of my research is to help leaders recognize the value added by employees who exhibit organizational citizenship behaviors, in addition to those expected as part of generic job descriptions, and to further the research of organizational citizenship behavior.

Your participation will involve answering a series of 60 questions regarding the perception of behaviors, job performance, teamwork, fairness, job satisfaction, rewards, and recognition as part of your daily work routine. Your participation in this study is voluntary. If you choose not to participate or to withdraw from the study at any time, either before, during or after the survey, you can do so without penalty or loss of benefit to yourself. The results of the research study may be published but your identity will remain confidential and your name will not be disclosed to any outside party. You will not be informed if your survey was or was not included in the published survey results.

In this research there are no expectations of any health or emotional risks to you.

Although there may be no direct benefit to you, a possible benefit of your participation is to have the opportunity to provide insight about the perception of employee productivity, job satisfaction, teamwork, and rewards in the healthcare industry. Your responses to the survey can help leadership understand the current processes and perceptions of recognition and rewards in the performance review process from within healthcare organizations.

If you have any questions or concerns about the research study, please call me at (xxx) xxx-xxxx or send an email to me at: xxxxxxx@xxxxxx.xxx.

As a participant in this study, you should understand the following:

1. You may decline to participate or withdraw from participation at any time without consequences by contacting Julie Griffin, by phone (xxx) xxx-xxxx, and returning any research materials, whether completed or not, and a copy of the Participant Withdrawal Form by e-mail to xxxxxxx@xxxxxx.xxx.
2. The survey is expected to take approximately 30 minutes to complete.
3. Your identity will be kept confidential.
4. Julie D. Griffin has thoroughly explained the

parameters of the research study and all of your
questions and concerns have been addressed.

5. Data will be stored in a secure and locked area to
which only Julie D. Griffin has access. The data
will be held for a period of three years from the
date of dissertation approval by the Dean of the
University of Phoenix, School of Advanced
Studies. The data will be destroyed properly,
through confidential and secure data destruction
services, three years from the date of the Dean's
approval.

6. The research results will be used for publication.

7. You may request information on how to obtain a
copy of the results at anytime by contacting Julie
D. Griffin at xxxxxxx@xxxxxx.xxx.

"By signing this form you acknowledge that you
understand the nature of the study, the potential risks
to you as a participant, your right to withdraw as a
study participant, and the means by which your
identity will be kept confidential. Your signature on
this form also indicates that you are 18 years old or
older and that you give your permission to voluntarily
serve as a participant in the study described."

Signature of the participant

_____ Date _____

Signature of the researcher

_/s/ *Julie D. Griffin*_____ Date _**3/5/2012**__

Study Participation Number: _____

*Note: The information for direct educational institution emails is
redacted on the previous pages for privacy.*

APPENDIX D – Participant Withdrawal Form

By signing this withdrawal form, I hereby
remove myself from the study entitled: *Leadership
Recognition of Organizational Citizenship Behaviors
in Performance Evaluations in Washington State
Healthcare Organizations.* I understand that my
identity will be protected, information collected as a
result of my participation will be kept confidential, and
that all documentation and electronic information will
be destroyed.

My signature below acknowledges my
intentions to withdraw from the study.

Signature of participant and Date

_____

Study Participation Number:

_____

_____

Reason for withdrawal (voluntary, not required):

_____

_____

E-mail this document to Julie D. Griffin at noted
address.

APPENDIX E – CONFIDENTIALITY STATEMENT

LEADERSHIP RECOGNITION OF ORGANIZATIONAL CITIZENSHIP BEHAVIORS IN PERFORMANCE EVALUATIONS IN WASHINGTON STATE HEALTHCARE ORGANIZATIONS

JULIE DIANE GRIFFIN

CONFIDENTIALITY STATEMENT

As a researcher working on the above research study at the University of Phoenix, I understand that I must maintain the confidentiality of all information concerning all research participants as required by law. Only the University of Phoenix Institutional Review Board may have access to this information.

"Confidential Information" of participants includes but is not limited to: names, characteristics, or other identifying information, questionnaire scores, ratings, incidental comments, other information accrued either directly or indirectly through contact with any participant, and/or any other information that by its nature would be considered confidential. In order to maintain the confidentiality of the information,

I hereby agree to refrain from discussing or disclosing any Confidential Information regarding research participants, to any individual who is not part of the above research study or in need of the information for the expressed purposes on the research program. This includes having a conversation regarding the research project or its participants in a place where such a discussion might be overheard; or discussing any Confidential Information in a way that would allow an unauthorized person to associate (either correctly or incorrectly) an identity with such information.

I further agree to store research records whether paper, electronic or otherwise in a secure locked location under my direct control or with

appropriate safe guards. I hereby further agree that if
I have to use the services of a third party to assist in
the research study, who will potentially have access
to any Confidential Information of participants, that I
will enter into an agreement with said third party prior
to using any of the services, which shall provide at a
minimum the confidential obligations set forth herein.

I agree that I will immediately report any
known or suspected breach of this confidentiality
statement regarding the above research project to the
University of Phoenix, Institutional Review Board.

/s/ *Julie D. Griffin*_   Julie D. Griffin
Signature of Researcher   Printed Name

01/10/2012_
Date

/s/ *William O'Donnell*   William O'Donnell, Ph.D.
Signature of Witness   Printed Name

01/10/2012
Date

APPENDIX F – LETTER OF REQUEST FOR

PERMISSION TO USE AN EXISTING SURVEY

November 7, 2011

My name is Julie Griffin. I am a University of Phoenix doctoral student working on my dissertation. In preparation for conducting the data collection process, I am writing to request permission to use your research instrument regarding organizational citizenship behaviors from your published dissertation titled, *Communication Satisfaction, Interactional Justice, and Organizational Citizenship Behaviors: Staff Perceptions in a University Environment,* pages 112-117, published and copyrighted by ProQuest LLC (June, 2008). Your research instrument will be a valuable tool for me to gather the data required to conduct my survey.

For my doctoral dissertation I am studying leadership recognition of organizational citizenship behaviors in the formal performance evaluation process. I want to determine if employee productivity, teamwork, job satisfaction, and rewards are related to leadership formally recognizing employees who exhibit organizational citizenship behaviors as part of the performance evaluation process. The significance of my research is to help leaders recognize the value added by employees who exhibit organizational citizenship behaviors, in addition to those expected as part of generic job descriptions, and to further the research of the organizational citizenship behavior.

I will be pleased if would review and sign the enclosed document that provides me the permission to use your survey instrument to complete my dissertation study. I have enclosed a pre-paid return FedEx envelope for your convenience in returning the document to me.

Thank you in advance for your assistance.

Julie D. Griffin
Enclosures (2)

APPENDIX G – PERMISSION TO USE AN

EXISTING SURVEY

Dear Ms. Griffin,

Thank you for your request for permission to use the research instrument regarding organizational citizenship behaviors from the dissertation titled, *Communication Satisfaction, Interactional Justice, and Organizational Citizenship Behaviors: Staff Perceptions in a University Environment,* pages 112-117, in your research study. I am willing to allow you to reproduce the instrument as outlined in your letter at no charge with the following understanding:

- You will use this survey only for your research study and will not sell or use it with any compensated management / curriculum development activities.
- You will include the copyright statement on all copies of the instrument.

- You will send your research study and one copy of reports, articles, and the like that make the use of the survey data promptly to my attention upon completion of your dissertation.

If these are acceptable terms and conditions, please indicate by signing two copies of this letter, one of each of our records. Best Wishes on your study,

Sincerely,

Signature of Survey Instrument Author

Date 11/15/11

I understand and agree to abide by the above terms and conditions.

Signature of Survey Instrument User

Date 11/07/11

APPENDIX H: Modified Research Instrument

Note: The survey instrument used was adapted from, *Communication Satisfaction, Interactional Justice, and Organizational Citizenship Behaviors: Staff Perceptions in a University Environment*, by William Fournier, Ph.D., 2008 (Copyright 2008: ProQuest).

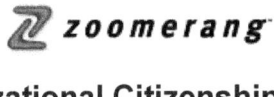

Organizational Citizenship Survey

Organizational Citizenship Survey

#_____

Page 1 - Question 1

Organizational Citizenship Behaviors are the behaviors YOU exhibit that are voluntary and go beyond your job description. Please rate YOURSELF on the following statements using the scale presented below. Check only one response per line:

	Very Dissatisfied	Dissatisfied	Neutral	Satisfied	Very Satisfied
Offers creative suggestions and unique ways of solving problems	○ 1	○ 2	○ 3	○ 4	○ 5
Makes creative suggestions to improve the overall quality of the department	○ 1	○ 2	○ 3	○ 4	○ 5
Shares creative suggestions for new ideas, products and/or services	○ 1	○ 2	○ 3	○ 4	○ 5
Shares creative suggestions regarding new and effective ways of performing job tasks	○ 1	○ 2	○ 3	○ 4	○ 5
Assists other employees when even your work-load is heavy	○ 1	○ 2	○ 3	○ 4	○ 5
Assists other employees regardless of who has the heavier work load	○ 1	○ 2	○ 3	○ 4	○ 5
Volunteers to help others with work when others are absent	○ 1	○ 2	○ 3	○ 4	○ 5
Takes the initiative to orient new employees to the department even though it is not required for your job	○ 1	○ 2	○ 3	○ 4	○ 5

Page 1 - Question 2

How satisfied are you with your job?

Very Dissatisfied	Dissatisfied	Neutral	Satisfied	Very Satisfied
○ 1	○ 2	○ 3	○ 4	○ 5

Page 1 - Question 3

In the last 90 days (three months), what has happened to your level of satisfaction in your job?

- ○ Decreased
- ○ Stayed the same
- ○ Increased

Page 2 - Question 4

Listed below are several types of information associated with a person's job. Please indicate your level of satisfaction with the amount and/or quality of each form of information ou have received from management over the past 90 days (three months):

	Very Dissatisfied	Dissatisfied	Neutral	Satisfied	Very Satisfied
Information about organizational policies and goals	○ 1	○ 2	○ 3	○ 4	○ 5
Information about how my job compares with others	○ 1	○ 2	○ 3	○ 4	○ 5
Information about how my performance is judged	○ 1	○ 2	○ 3	○ 4	○ 5
Recognition and rewards for my efforts	○ 1	○ 2	○ 3	○ 4	○ 5
Information about department policies and goals	○ 1	○ 2	○ 3	○ 4	○ 5
Information about employee benefits and pay	○ 1	○ 2	○ 3	○ 4	○ 5
Information regarding achievements and/or failures of the organization	○ 1	○ 2	○ 3	○ 4	○ 5
Extent to which the organization's communication motivates me to meet its goals	○ 1	○ 2	○ 3	○ 4	○ 5
Extent to which communication within my organization makes me identify with it or feel like a vital part of the organization	○ 1	○ 2	○ 3	○ 4	○ 5
Extent to which the communication in my organization is interesting and helpful to me	○ 1	○ 2	○ 3	○ 4	○ 5

(Page 2, Question 4, continued)

Extent to which I receive the information necessary to do my job	○ 1	○ 2	○ 3	○ 4	○ 5
Extent to which conflicts are handled appropriately through proper communications and channels	○ 1	○ 2	○ 3	○ 4	○ 5
Extent to which the "grapevine" is active and useful in my organization	○ 1	○ 2	○ 3	○ 4	○ 5
Extent to which communication with other employees at my level within the organization is accurate and free-flowing	○ 1	○ 2	○ 3	○ 4	○ 5
Extent to which my work-group and team is compatible	○ 1	○ 2	○ 3	○ 4	○ 5
Extent to which our meetings are well organized	○ 1	○ 2	○ 3	○ 4	○ 5
Extent to which reports are clear and concise	○ 1	○ 2	○ 3	○ 4	○ 5
Extent to which attitudes toward communications are healthy	○ 1	○ 2	○ 3	○ 4	○ 5
Extent to which informal communication is active and accurate	○ 1	○ 2	○ 3	○ 4	○ 5

Page 3 - Question 5

How would you rate your productivity in your job?

Very Low	Low	Average	High	Very High
○ 1	○ 2	○ 3	○ 4	○ 5

Page 3 - Question 6

In the last 90 days (three months) what has happened to your productivity?

- ○ Decreased
- ○ Stayed the same
- ○ Increased

Page 3 - Question 7

Procedural Justice refers to the perception of fairness we feel when we consider the process used by our supervisor to make decisions. We make decisions and perform our jobs based on whether the decisions and feedback from our supervisor were fair, consistent, and justified. Please indicate your perception of the feedback from your supervisor over the past 90 days (three months) for each of the following:

	label	label	label	label	label
Used consistent standards in evaluating your performance	○ 1	○ 2	○ 3	○ 4	○ 5
Showed a real interest in trying to be fair	○ 1	○ 2	○ 3	○ 4	○ 5
Took into account factors beyond your control	○ 1	○ 2	○ 3	○ 4	○ 5
Obtained accurate information about your performance	○ 1	○ 2	○ 3	○ 4	○ 5
Allowed personal motives or bias to influence recommendations	○ 1	○ 2	○ 3	○ 4	○ 5
Was influenced by things that should not have been considered	○ 1	○ 2	○ 3	○ 4	○ 5
Provided support for a raise or promotion	○ 1	○ 2	○ 3	○ 4	○ 5

Page 3 - Question 8

Interactional Justice refers to the perceptions of fairness we feel when interacting with our organization, managers, and/or supervisors. We make decisions about whether we were treated with respect and truthfulness, and if decisions made by our leaders were justified. Please indicate the extent to which your managers/supervisors have provided the following over the past 90 days (three months):

	Never	Rarely	Sometimes	Almost Always	Always
Provided rewards and recognition for a job well done	O 1	O 2	O 3	O 4	O 5
Was honest and ethical interacting with me	O 1	O 2	O 3	O 4	O 5
Provided opportunities for me to express myself	O 1	O 2	O 3	O 4	O 5
Considered my view regarding my performance	O 1	O 2	O 3	O 4	O 5
Provided helpful feedback	O 1	O 2	O 3	O 4	O 5
Provided candid and honest feedback	O 1	O 2	O 3	O 4	O 5
Exhibited a thorough familiarity with my performance	O 1	O 2	O 3	O 4	O 5
Asked for my input before submitting a recommendation	O 1	O 2	O 3	O 4	O 5
Clearly defined what is expected of me	O 1	O 2	O 3	O 4	O 5
Discussed plans and objectives to improve my performance	O 1	O 2	O 3	O 4	O 5
Asked me to evaluate my job performance	O 1	O 2	O 3	O 4	O 5
Asked me how I believe I could improve my job performance	O 1	O 2	O 3	O 4	O 5
Frequently observed my job performance	O 1	O 2	O 3	O 4	O 5

Page 3 - Question 9

Did you receive a major personal performance reward or major recognition in the last 90 days (three months)? If so, please select from one of the following, or choose no.

- Raise in pay
- Job title promotion
- Raise in pay and job title promotion
- No

Page 4 - Question 10

Please provide the following demographic information. Your identity and responses are confidential. This information will only be used for describing general differences between the various levels of demographics. Gender

- Male
- Female
- Decline to answer

Page 4 - Question 11

Age

- 18 or below
- 19-29
- 30-39
- 40-49
- 50-59
- 60 or older
- Decline to answer

Page 4 - Question 12

Level of Education

○ Did not finish high school
○ High school
○ Some college, no degree
○ Two year college degree
○ Four year college degree
○ Graduate degree
○ Post-graduate degree
○ Decline to answer

Page 4 - Question 13

Salary Range (annually)

○ Less than $20,000
○ $21,000 - $29,000
○ $30,000 - $39,000
○ $40,000 - $49,000
○ $50,000 - $59,000
○ $60,000 - $69,000
○ $70,000 - $80,000
○ $80,000 or more
○ Decline to answer

Page 4 - Question 14

Length of time in current position

○ Less than 1 year
○ 1 - 5 years
○ 6 - 10 years
○ 11 - 15 years
○ 16 - 20 years
○ 21 - 25 years
○ 26 years or more
○ Decline to answer

Page 4 - Question 15

Current position

○ Non-management
○ Management
○ Administrative
○ Licensed Medical Personnel
○ Decline to answer

Page 4 - Question 16

Job status

○ Full-time
○ Part-time
○ On-call
○ Temporary
○ Decline to answer

Page 4 - Question 17

Please provide a simple code word only you would know, and that you will remember. You will need to provide this code word to the researcher for participant verification should you contact the researcher in the future.

Page 4 – Question 18

Please select the type of medical facility in which you are employed (choose the one best answer)

○ Major Hospital
○ Mental Health Facility
○ Assisted Living/Nursing Facility
○ Medical Office – Adults
○ Dental Office
○ Chiropractic Office
○ Medical Laboratory
○ Physical Therapy/Rehabilitation Facility
○ Medical Office – Pediatrics
○ Urgent Care Medical Facility
○ Other (not included in list above)

APPENDIX I – SURVEY CONSTRUCTS

Table 4 - Construct of Questions and Number of Items

Construct	Number of Items	Survey Question(s)
Leadership Recognition	20	32 to 51
OCBs	4	5 to 8
Productivity	11	14 to20, 22 to 24, 30
Teamwork	5	1 to 4, 25
Job Performance	8	11 to 13, 21, 26 to 29
Satisfaction	1	9

* Questions 10 and 31 are not significant to the outcome of data analysis as they did not conform to the Likert-type scale for remaining survey questions.

INDEX

CURRICULUM VITAE

Julie D. Conzelmann, D.M.
Camano Island, WA

julie.conzelmann@gmail.com
www.superioreditingservices.com

MANAGER
BUSINESS LEADER
DEAN
MENTOR
CERTIFIED COPYEDITOR

TEACHING PHILOSOPHY STATEMENT

The basis for my teaching philosophy is the
material I teach, relevance to scholarship, the lessons
I learn from personal successes and failures working
with students, and student feedback. I love to engage
students in a respectful forum of learning and
individual discovery. I enjoy hearing the excitement in
students' testimonials regarding learning and
mastering skills that transformed students' practices
and perspectives – and when they say I made a
difference in the students' success! I not only count
these milestones as my teaching successes, but also

make it a habit to have students reflect on the beginning of their educational journey and the work each student put into obtaining their goals.

A student-oriented teaching environment promotes purposeful and enduring learning. My responsibility is to know my students, the strengths and weaknesses each individual contributes to the group, and students' goals. By assessing the students' needs, I can tailor the curriculum to fit the needs and goals, but also provide a challenging environment wherein students emerge with new knowledge and inspiration to continue to be a life-long learner. This educational environment is the foundation needed for students to build connections between inherent knowledge and tacit knowledge.

I embrace teaching and mentoring because these activities stimulate intellectual camaraderie, argumentation, and cooperative problem solving and lay the groundwork for life-long collaborative practice. I demonstrate curiosity and passion about a subject area to motivate students to learn, teach among colleagues whose scholarship and expertise are complementary to mine. Collaborating with enthusiastic faculty rooted in servant and transformational leadership models how to enhance scholarship, teaching, and learning through diversity and teamwork. Teaching and mentoring brings great joy to my life, fulfilling a desire to leave the world in a better state:

*"To leave the world a bit better, whether by a
healthy child, a garden patch, or a redeemed
social condition; to know that even one life has
breathed easier because you have lived - that
is to have succeeded"*
~Ralph Waldo Emerson

SUMMARY OF EXPERIENCE

Detail-oriented business leader with more than
30 years of experience holding positions from a
deputy director, financial officer, and a project
specialist, to a tutor for students and founder of my
own successful editing business. Provides leadership
experience to management, as advisor, or instructor
supporting a academics in organizational
management, business management, organizational
leadership, or assisting students with academic
writing skills.

PROFESSIONAL EXPERIENCE

Eidyia University   Columbus, OH   2015 - Present
Dean of Liberal Arts

- Provide voluntary leadership in the creation and
  building of Eidyia Institute to open in 2016
- Create standardized documents for all Deans and
  instructors including course syllabus; curriculum

map; formatted student paper for writing
assignments; peer, instructor, and self-evaluation
documents; mission, vision, and goal statement;
and 20-year strategic outline
- Take notes and type leadership meeting minutes in
absence of administrative staff
- Created curriculum for future instruction of
copyediting certification course
- Assist executive leadership select, interview, and
retain leadership and instructional staff

Superior Editing Services **Founder/Owner**	**Camano Island, WA**	**2012 – Present**

- Created and managed business model and launch,
generating 75 clients within the first year of
operation
- Edit, proofread, and format >200 college-level
academic papers (theses and dissertations), at
least five journal articles, approximately six
children's books, and three novels annually
- Consult / mentor >200 graduate and post-graduate
students and authors annually for writing,
formatting, and goal setting
- Built / maintain website:
www.superioreditingservices.com

Bellingham   **Bellingham, WA**   **2011 – 2012**
Technical College
Tutor and Proctor

- Assisted >30 college students per semester with accounting, statistics, and college-level writing
- Proctored >10 tests and examinations each semester
- Edited, proofread, and formatted approximately eight college-level academic papers per semester

TriWest Healthcare   **Phoenix, AZ**   **2007 – 2010**
Alliance
Project Specialist I

- Compiled, analyzed, researched, edited, and summarized information and facts using standard business English, for >1,000 reports, department projects, and correspondence in support of 100+ research projects, summary reports, and bid activities annually
- Managed the division budget of more than $12M
- Researched and compiled >30 leadership reports and presentations annually for department vice-president and directors including company board and internal committees

Board of   **Phoenix, AZ**   **2009 – 2009**
Psychologist
Examiners
State of Arizona
Deputy Director

- Managed, reviewed, recommended, and granted licensure applications to psychologist applicants for the state
- Supervised 20 employees and >20 scheduled monthly Application Review Committee meetings
- Reviewed >200 educational transcripts, applications, and continuing education credit (CEC) verifications monthly

Arizona Board of   **Phoenix, AZ**   **2004 – 2007**
Technical
Registration
Administrative Services Officer II

- Represented Board as financial officer, procurement, security, and Information Technology manager
- Created biennial budget; managed and oversaw accounting, revenues, and expenditures
- Researched and wrote legislative rules; met with Governor's Regulatory Rules Commission

QSI Specialists   Las Vegas, NV   2002 – 2004
Mystery Shopper

- Researched and investigated more than 1,000 businesses and employees under supervision of licensed private investigator; scheduled shops for daily completion
- Wrote >20 detailed reports monthly, listing investigations and findings

Southern Nevada   Las Vegas, NV   2000 – 2004
Health District
Senior Administrative Assistant

- Responsible for grant writing; managing of grant funds of >$1M
- Managed three volunteer staff members; managed grant research, accounting, and as representative at health fairs

EDUCATION

- Doctor of Management in Organizational Leadership University of Phoenix, 08/12
- Master of Business Administration, University of Phoenix, 06/08
- Bachelors in Business Administration (Human Resources minor), Saint Leo University, 04/07

TRAINING / CERTIFICATIONS

• Certified Copyeditor, University of California, San
Diego Extension, 06/15

PUBLICATIONS

Griffin, J. D. (2015). Leadership Recognition of
Organizational Leadership Behaviors in
Performance Evaluations in Washington State
Healthcare Organizations. Virginia Beach, VA:
D. Boyer Consulting.
Griffin, J. D. (2012). Leadership Recognition of
Organizational Leadership Behaviors in
Performance Evaluations in Washington State
Healthcare Organizations, ProQuest.

EDITED PUBLICATIONS

Lopez, J. A. (2015). The Distance Learning Model.
Society for Advancement of Management, Inc.
Quade, K. (2014). *Dynamical Boards*. Amazon.
Quade, K. (2014). *Simple Rules for Complex Times*.
Amazon.
Ruscyzk, L. (2014). *Charlie the Cavalier Travels the
World*. B00OBWM2ZY. Charlie the Cavalier:
Lockhaven, PA.

Wieters, L., Torres, E., McCabe, C., & Hirschberg, K. (2015). *Building Organizational Resilience in SMEs. Journal of Small Business Management.* (Forthcoming)

SKILLS AND QUALIFICATIONS

- Expert in APA, MLA & Chicago Editing
- Budget Development & Management
- Business Ethics
- Communications & Writing Training
- Entrepreneurship
- General Accounting & GAAP Laws
- Grant Writing
- Human Resources Management
- Inventory Control & Procurement
- Marketing
- Mentoring
- MS Office Expert
- Policy Development & Updates
- Public Speaking & Presentations
- Training & Development

AWARDS AND RECOGNITION

- Dean's List, Saint Leo University, 01/05/06

PROFESSIONAL AFFILIATIONS

- Member, Association of Copy Editors Society, 2015 – present
- Member, The National Association of Independent Writers and Editors, 2014 – present
- Member, Editorial Freelancers Association, 2012 – present,

ABOUT THE AUTHOR

Dr. Julie Conzelmann has an extensive
background in writing and editing to include grant
writing; creating, editing, and revising legislative
statutes; correspondence and communications for a
Department of Defense contractor; and 12 years of
academic writing. These extensive combined
experiences were the impetus to start Superior
Editing Services. She has edited in every genre of

writing. At the time of this publication, Julie is writing a compilation of humorous stories, a book about academic writing, and collaborating on a children's book.

Julie is married to her high school sweetheart after a 30-year separation and two-year courtship. She is the mother of two biological children, Eric and Elisabeth, and three bonus children, Shannon, Breanne, and Travis, all of whom have made her proud and are the joy of her heart.

When not editing or writing, Julie enjoys going for walks with her husband on the trails and beaches near their home on Camano Island, Washington. Photography is a special hobby Julie enjoys. She photographs animals and other natural beauty – especially bald eagles and other birds – and offers copyrighted prints through her website Conzelmann Castle Photography.

Follow Dr. Conzelmann on Social Media or Subscribe to Her Business Pages

Julie.conzelmann@gmail.com

Contact Julie to inquire about opportunities for university faculty positions or to obtain editorial assistance with writing and editing for novelists. Offering certified specialist knowledge and skills for academic thesis or dissertation editing.

Business Website: http://www.superioreditingservices.com

LinkedIn Profile: https://www.linkedin.com/in/juliegriffin1

Facebook Business Page:
https://www.facebook.com/superioreditingservices

Twitter: http://www.Twitter.com/Dr_Conzelmann

ABOUT THE BOOK

The Leadership Recognition Of Organizational Citizenship Behaviors In Performance Evaluations In Washington State Healthcare Organizations research study provides an important perspective of the benefits of managers and leaders recognizing the exemplary performance of employees. Recognizing the unexpected performance and behaviors exhibited by employees strengthens the employee-employer bond.

The statistics speak for themselves. Though this research study focuses on the health industry, the conclusions and findings of this study can be attributed throughout corporate America to any industry, field, or work environment.

Publishing Services
Virginia Beach, VA 23464

http://dboyerconsulting.com
Dawn@DBoyerConsulting.com

KEY TERMS: altruism, American Statistical Association, attitudes, authoritarianism, behavioral management / behavioral models / behavioral theories, behavioral models, behavioral theories, benchmarking, best practices, business management, charismatic leadership, civic virtue, cognitive theory, competencies, construct validity, covariance analysis, cultural chaos, cultural development, cultural model, democracy, discretionary behaviors, emotional intelligence, employee recognition, Enterprise Resource Planning (ERP), environmental analysis, environmental leadership, equity theory, functionalism, global societies, good citizen syndrome, High-Performance Work Systems (HPWS), human behavior, human capital, Human Resources Management (HRM), incentives, independent variables, intellectual stimulation, interactional justice, intrinsic behaviors, knowledge skills and abilities (KSA), leader-follower relationship, leadership recognition, leadership style, leadership theories, management theories, mechanistic behavioral model, mentoring, modeling, motivational leadership, motivational theory, multiple-regression analysis, operant reinforcement, operational design, operational systems, organismic biology, organizational behavior, Organizational Citizenship Behaviors (OCB), organizational culture index, Organizational Leadership, participative management theory, Pearson t-tests, peer networks, performance appraisal, performance inequality, performance management, personality traits, qualitative research, quantitative analysis, relationship-based variables, scientific methods, self-efficacy, situational leadership theory, social behavior modeling, social behaviors, social constructionist theory, social exchange theory, social psychology behavior, social-exchange, social-identity, statistical analysis, Succession planning, theory of relationships, Total Quality Management (TQM), transformational leadership, value-added benefit, workforce analysis